KNOW YOUR BENEFITS

MW01127293

Federal Benefits for Veterans Dependents and Survivors

2015 Supplemental · Updates 2014 edition

VA | U.S. Department of Veterans Affairs

i

Introduction

(**Editor's Note:** *This booklet is a brief overview of the most commonly sought information concerning Veterans Benefits. This publication updates the* **2014 Benefits for Veterans, Dependents and Survivors** *handbook by correcting information such as cost of living adjustments and newly offered programs. For the most accurate information, Veterans and family members should visit the websites provided within this publication as regulations, payments and eligibility requirements are subject to change.)*

Veterans of the United States armed forces may be eligible for a broad range of benefits and services provided by the U.S. Department of Veterans Affairs (VA). These benefits are codified in Title 38 of the United States Code. This booklet contains the most commonly requested VA benefits and services. For additional information, please visit **www.va.gov** and review a hardcopy of The Federal Benefits for Veterans, Dependents and Survivors benefits book.

General Eligibility: Eligibility for most VA benefits is based upon discharge from active military service under other than dishonorable conditions. Active service means full-time service, other than active duty for training, as a member of the Army, Navy, Air Force, Marine Corps, Coast Guard, or as a commissioned officer of the Public Health Service, Environmental Science Services Administration or National Oceanic and Atmospheric Administration, or its predecessor, the Coast and Geodetic Survey. Dishonorable and bad conduct discharges issued by general courts-martial may bar VA benefits. Veterans in prison must contact VA to determine eligibility. VA benefits will not be provided to any Veteran or dependent wanted for an outstanding felony warrant.

Important Documents: In order to expedite benefits delivery, Veterans seeking a VA benefit for the first time must submit a copy of their service discharge form (DD-214, DD-215, or for World War II Veterans, a WD form).

VA facilities: To find a VA facility nearest you, go to **http://www. va.gov/directory/guide/division.asp?dnum=1&isFlash=0**.

eBenefits

Through eBenefits Veterans can: apply for benefits, view their disability compensation claim status, access official military personnel documents (e.g., DD Form 214, Certificate of Release or Discharge from Active Duty), transfer entitlement of Post-9/11 GI Bill to eligible dependents (Servicemembers only), obtain a VA-guaranteed home loan Certificate of Eligibility, and register for and update direct deposit information for certain benefits. New features are added regularly.

Accessing eBenefits: The portal is located at **www.ebenefits. va.gov.** Servicemembers or Veterans must register for an eBenefits account at one of two levels: Basic or Premium. A Premium account allows the user to access personal data in VA and DoD systems, as well as apply for benefits online, check the status of claims and more. The Basic account limits the self-service features that can be accessed.

To register for an account, Veterans must be listed in the Defense Enrollment Eligibility Reporting System (DEERS) and obtain a DoD Self Service (DS) Logon. Servicemembers can access eBenefits with a DS Logon or Common Access Card (CAC). They can choose from two levels of registration: DS Logon Level 1 (Basic) and DS Logon Level 2 (Premium). A DS Logon is an identity (user name and password) that is used by various DoD and VA Websites, including eBenefits. Those registered in DEERS are eligible for a DS Logon. A DS Logon is valid for the rest of your life.

Identity verification: Many people will be able to verify their identity online by answering a few security questions. A few may need to visit a VA regional office or TRICARE Service Center to have their identities verified. Servicemembers may verify their identity online by using their CAC.Military retirees may verify their identity online using their Defense Finance and Accounting Service (DFAS) Logon. Veterans in receipt of VA benefits via direct deposit may have their identity verified by calling 1-800-827-1000 and selecting option 7.

Contents

Health Care Benefits

For additional information on VA health care, visit: **www.va.gov/ health** as well as **VHA's 2015 Health Care Benefits Overview** – a guide designed to provide Veterans and their families with the information they need to understand VA's health care system.

Basic Eligibility: A person who served in the active military, naval, or air service and who was discharged or released under conditions other than dishonorable may qualify for VA health care benefits including qualifying Reserve and National Guard members.

Minimum Duty Requirements: Veterans who enlisted after Sept. 7, 1980, or who entered active duty after Oct. 16, 1981, must have served 24 continuous months or the full period for which they were called to active duty in order to be eligible. This minimum duty requirement may not apply to Veterans discharged for hardship, early out or a disability incurred or aggravated in the line of duty.

Enrollment: For most Veterans, entry into the VA health care system begins by applying for enrollment. Veterans can now apply and submit their application (VA Form 1010EZ), online at **http://www.va.gov/ vaforms/form_detail.asp?formno=10ez**. If assistance is needed for the online enrollment form, an online chat representative is available to answer questions Monday – Friday, between 8 a.m. and 8 p.m. EST. Veterans can also enroll by calling 1-877-222-8387, Monday through Friday, 8 a.m. to 8 p.m. EST, or at any VA health care facility or VA regional office. Once enrolled, Veterans can receive health care at VA health care facilities anywhere in the country.

The following four categories of Veterans are not required to enroll, but are urged to do so to permit better planning of health resources:
1. Veterans with a service-connected disability of 50 percent or more.
2. Veterans seeking care for a disability the military determined was incurred or aggravated in the line of duty, but which VA has not yet rated, within 12 months of discharge.
3. Veterans seeking care for a service-connected disability only.
4. Veterans seeking registry examinations (Ionizing Radiation, Agent Orange, Gulf War/Operation Enduring Freedom/ Operation Iraqi Freedom/ Operation New Dawn (OEF/OIF/ OND) depleted uranium, airborne hazards and Airborne Hazards and Open Burn Pit Registry).

Priority Groups: During enrollment, each Veteran is assigned to a priority group. VA uses priority groups to balance demand for VA health care enrollment with resources. Changes in available resources may reduce the number of priority groups VA can enroll. If this occurs, VA will publicize the changes and notify affected enrollees. A description of priority groups follows:

Group 1: Veterans with service-connected disabilities rated 50 percent or more and/or Veterans determined by VA to be unemployable due to service-connected conditions.
Group 2: Veterans with service-connected disabilities rated 30 or 40 percent.
Group 3: Veterans who are former prisoners of war (POWs).
   Veterans awarded the Purple Heart medal.
   Veterans awarded the Medal of Honor.
   Veterans whose discharge was for a disability incurred or aggravated in the line of duty.
   Veterans with VA service-connected disabilities rated 10 percent or 20 percent.
   Veterans awarded special eligibility classification under Title 38, U.S.C., § 1151, "benefits for individuals disabled by treatment or vocational rehabilitation."
Group 4: Veterans receiving increased compensation or pension based
   on their need for regular aid and attendance or by reason of being permanently housebound.
   Veterans determined by VA to be catastrophically disabled.
Group 5: Nonservice-connected Veterans and noncompensable service-
   connected Veterans rated 0 percent, whose annual income and/or net worth are not greater than VA financial thresholds.
   Veterans receiving VA Pension benefits.
   Veterans eligible for Medicaid benefits.
Group 6: Compensable 0 percent service-connected Veterans.
   Veterans exposed to ionizing radiation during atmospheric testing or during the occupation of Hiroshima and Nagasaki.
   Project 112/SHAD participants.
   Veterans who served in the Republic of Vietnam between Jan. 9, 1962 and May 7, 1975.
   Veterans who served in the Southwest Asia theater of operations from Aug. 2, 1990, through Nov. 11, 1998.
   Veterans who served in a theater of combat operations after

Nov. 11, 1998, as follows:

Veterans discharged from active duty on or after Jan. 28, 2003, for five years post discharge;

Veterans who served on active duty at Camp Lejeune, N.C., for no

fewer than 30 days beginning Jan. 1, 1957, and ending Dec. 31, 1987.

Group 7: Veterans with incomes below the geographic means test income

thresholds and who agree to pay the applicable copayment.

Group 8: Veterans with gross household incomes above VA national income threshold and the geographically-adjusted income threshold for their resident location and who agree to pay copayments. Veterans eligible for enrollment: Noncompensable 0-percent service-connected:

Subpriority a: Enrolled as of Jan. 16, 2003, and who have remained enrolled since that date and/or placed in this subpriority due to changed eligibility status.

Subpriority b: Enrolled on or after June 15, 2009, whose income exceeds the current VA national income thresholds or VA national geographic income thresholds by 10 percent or less

Veterans eligible for enrollment: nonservice-connected and

Subpriority c: Enrolled as of Jan. 16, 2003, and who remained enrolled since that date and/ or placed in this subpriority due to changed eligibility status

Subpriority d: Enrolled on or after June 15, 2009 whose income exceeds the current VA national income thresholds or VA national geographic income thresholds by 10 percent or less

Veterans NOT eligible for enrollment: Veterans not meeting the criteria above:

Subpriority e: Noncompensable 0-percent service-connected

Subpriority f: Nonservice-connected

VA's income thresholds change annually and current levels can be located at: http://nationalincomelimits.vaftl.us/.

Veterans Choice Program

As directed by the Veterans Access, Choice and Accountability Act of 2014, VA implemented the Veterans Choice Program, which will operate for 3 years or until the Fund is exhausted. The program allows certain eligible Veterans to elect to receive care from non-VA health care providers if they cannot receive VA care within 30 days or live more than 40 miles from a VA facility or face excessive travel burdens.

VA will also extend the Assisted Living Pilot Program for Veterans with Traumatic Brain Injury for 3 years, through October 6, 2017. This program assesses the effectiveness of providing assisted living services to eligible Veterans with traumatic brain injuries to "enhance the rehabilitation, quality of life, and community integration of such Veterans."

Under the Act, Veterans can receive counseling and appropriate care and services required to overcome psychological trauma resulting from military sexual trauma (MST) that occurred while the Veteran was serving on inactive duty training (such as drill weekends for members of the Reserves and National Guard). Such benefits are provided at no cost to the Veteran.

The Choice Act also authorizes VA, in consultation with the Department of Defense (DoD), to provide MST-related care and services to members of the Armed Forces on active duty (including members of the National Guard and Reserves) without the need for a referral from a TRICARE provider or a military treatment facility. VA is working with DoD on implementation of this benefit.

Women Veterans: Women Veterans are eligible for the same VA benefits as male Veterans. Comprehensive health services are available to women Veterans including primary care, specialty care, mental health care, residential treatment and reproductive health care services. VA provides management of acute and chronic illnesses, preventive care, contraceptive and gynecology services, menopause management, and cancer screenings, including pap smears and mammograms.

Maternity care is covered in the Medical Benefits package. Women Veterans can receive maternity care from an OB/GYN, family practitioner, or certified nurse midwife who provides pregnancy care. VA covers the costs of care for newborn children of women Veterans for seven days after birth. Infertility evaluation and limited treatments are also available.

Women Veterans Program Managers are available at all VA facilities to assist women Veterans in their health care and benefits. For more information, visit **http://www.womenshealth.va.gov/**.

Lesbian Gay Bisexual and Transgender (LGBT) Veterans: LGBT Veterans are eligible for the same VA benefits as any other Veteran and will be treated in a welcoming environment. Transgender Veterans will be treated based upon their self-identified gender, including room assignments in residential and inpatient settings. Same-Sex Couples: VA launched a new website to inform Veterans and beneficiaries of the recent changes in the law and procedures involving same-sex marriages. Veterans can learn more about VA's guidance regarding same-sex marriages at **www.va.gov/opa/marriage**.

Military Sexual Trauma: Military sexual trauma (MST) is the term that VA uses to refer to sexual assault or repeated, threatening sexual harassment that occurred while a Veteran was serving on active duty (or active duty for training if the service was in the National Guard or Reserve). VA health care professionals provide counseling and treatment to help Veterans overcome health issues related to MST. Veterans who are not otherwise eligible for VA health care may still receive these services. For additional information, visit: **http://www.mentalhealth.va.gov/msthome.asp**.

Presumptive Eligibility for Psychosis and Other Mental Illness: Certain Veterans who experienced psychosis within a specified time-frame are to have their psychosis presumed to be service-connected for purposes of VA medical benefits.

Psychosis: Eligibility for treatment of psychosis, and such condition is exempted from copayments for any Veteran who served in the United States active duty military, naval, or air service and developed such psychosis within two years after discharge or release from the active military duty, naval or air service; and before the following date associated with the war or conflict in which the Veteran served: Mental Illness (other than Psychosis): Eligibility for benefits is established for treatment of an active mental illness (other than psychosis), and such condition is exempted from copayments for any Veteran of the Persian Gulf War who developed such mental illness:

a. Within two years after discharge or release from the active duty military, naval, or air service; and

b. Before the end of the two-year period beginning on the last day of the Persian Gulf War (end date not yet determined).

OEF/OIF/OND Care Management: Each VA medical center has an Operation Enduring Freedom/Operation Iraqi Freedom/Operation New Dawn (OEF/OIF/OND) Care Management team in place to coordinate patient care activities and ensure that Servicemembers and Veterans are receiving patient-centered, integrated care and benefits. More information for connecting with OEF/OIF/OND Care Management teams can be found at **www.oefoif.va.gov**.

Key Information for Veterans about the Affordable Care Act /Health Care Law
- Veterans who are enrolled in VA health care don't need to take additional steps to meet the health care law coverage standards.
- The health care law does not change VA health benefits or Veterans' out-of-pocket costs.
- Veterans who are not enrolled in VA health care can apply at any time.

For additional information about VA and the health care law, visit **www.va.gov/aca** or call 1-877-222-VETS (8387).

Financial Assessment: Most Veterans not receiving VA disability compensation or pension payments must provide a financial assessment, also known as a means test, upon initial application to determine whether they are below VA income thresholds. VA is currently not enrolling new applicants who decline to provide financial information unless they have a special eligibility factor exempting them from disclosure. VA's income thresholds are located at **http://nationalincomelimits.vaftl.us/**.

As of 2014, VA no longer requires enrolled non-service connected and 0-percent non-compensable service connected Veterans to provide their financial information annually. A means test will continue to be collected from Veterans at the time of application for enrollment. In lieu of the annual financial reporting, VA will confirm the Veteran's financial information using information obtained from the Internal Revenue Service and Social Security Administration.

Medical Services and Medication Copayments: Some Veterans are required to make copayments (copays) to receive VA health care and/or medications.

Inpatient Care: Priority Group 7 and certain other Veterans are responsible for paying 20 percent of VA's inpatient copay, which totals $243.20 for the first 90 days of inpatient hospital care during any 365-day period. For each additional 90-day period, the charge is $121.60. In addition, there is a $2 per diem charge. Copay amounts may change on an annual basis.

Priority Group 8 and certain other Veterans are responsible for VA's inpatient copay, which totals $1,216 for the first 90 days of care during any 365-day period. For each additional 90-day period, the charge is $608. In addition, there is a $10 per diem charge. Copay amounts may change on an annual basis.

Extended Care Services: Veterans may be subject to a copay for extended care services. The copay amount is based on the Veteran's available resources and is determined by a calculation using the financial information from VA Form 10-10EC, Application for Extended Care Services. The copay can range from $0 to a maximum copay amount of $97 a day.

Outpatient Care: While many Veterans qualify for free health care services based on a VA compensable service-connected condition or other qualifying factor, most Veterans are asked to provide a financial assessment, to determine if they qualify for free services. Veterans whose income exceeds the established VA Income Thresholds, as well as those who choose not to complete the financial assessment, must agree to pay required copays to become eligible for VA health care services.
　　Primary Care Services: $15
　　Specialty Care Services: $50

NOTE: The copay amount is limited to a single charge per visit regardless of the number of health care providers seen in a single day. The copay amount is based on the highest level of clinical service received. Certain services are not charged a copay. Copays do not apply to publicly announced VA health fairs or outpatient visits solely for preventive screening and/or vaccinations.

Medication Copays: While many Veterans are exempt for medication copays, nonservice-connected Veterans in Priority Groups 7 and 8 are charged $9 for each 30-day or less supply of medication provided on an outpatient basis for the treatment of a nonservice-connected condition. Veterans enrolled in Priority Groups 2 through

6 are charged $8 for each 30-day or less supply of medication; the maximum copay for medications that will be charged in calendar year 2013 is $960 for nonservice-connected medications.

NOTE: Copays apply to prescription and over-the-counter medications, such as aspirin, cough syrup or vitamins dispensed by a VA pharmacy. Copays are not charged for medical supplies, such as syringes or alcohol wipes. Copays do not apply to condoms. Health Savings Accounts: (HSAs) can be utilized to make VA copayments. HSAs are usually linked to High Deductible Health Plans (HDHPs).

Private Health Insurance Billing: VA is required to bill private health insurance providers for medical care, supplies and medications provided for treatment of Veterans' nonservice-connected conditions. Generally, VA cannot bill Medicare but can bill Medicare supplemental health insurance and/or TRICARE for Life (TFL) for covered services. VA is authorized to bill and accept reimbursement from High Deductible Health Plans (HDHPs) for care provided for nonservice-connected conditions.VA may also accept reimbursement from Health Reimbursement Arrangements (HRAs) for care provided for nonservice-connected conditions.

Reimbursement of Travel Costs: Eligible Veterans and non-veterans may be provided mileage reimbursement or, when medically indicated, special mode transport (e.g., wheelchair van, ambulance), when travel is in relation to VA medical care. Mileage reimbursement is 41.5 cents per mile and is subject to a deductible of $3 for each one-way trip and $6 for a round trip; with a maximum deductible of $18 or the amount after six one-way trips (whichever occurs first) per calendar month. The deductible may be waived when travel is; in relation to a VA compensation or pension examination; by a special mode of transportation; by an eligible non-veteran; or will cause a severe financial hardship, as defined by current regulatory guidelines.

Eligibility: The following are eligible for VA travel benefits:
Veterans rated 30 percent or more service-connected.
Veterans traveling for treatment of service-connected.
conditions.
Veterans who receive a VA pension.
Veterans traveling for scheduled compensation or pension.
examinations.

Veterans whose income does not exceed the maximum.
annual VA pension rate.
Veterans in certain emergency situations.
Veterans whose medical condition requires a special mode of
transportation and travel is pre-authorized. (Advanced
authorization is not required in an emergency, and a delay
would be hazardous to life or health).
Certain non-veterans when related to care of a Veteran
(caregivers, attendants, donors and other claimants subject to
current regulatory guidelines)

Reporting Fraud: Help VA's Secretary ensure integrity by report-
ing suspected fraud, waste or abuse in VA programs or operations.
Report fraud to:
VA Inspector General Hotline
810 Vermont Ave., NW
Washington, D.C. 20420E-mail: vaoighotline@va.gov
VAOIG hotline 1-800-488-8244
Fax: (202) 495-5861

Veteran Health Registries: Certain Veterans can participate in a
VA health registry and receive free evaluations. VA maintains health
registries to provide special health evaluations and health-related
information. To participate, contact the Environmental Health Coordinator at the nearest VA health care facility or visit **www.publichealth.
va.gov/exposures** to see a directory which lists Environmental
Health Coordinators by state and U.S. territory. Veterans should be
aware that a health registry evaluation is not a disability compensation exam. A registry evaluation does not start a claim for compensation and is not required for any VA benefits.

Gulf War Registry: For Veterans who served on active military
duty in Southwest Asia during the Gulf War, which began in 1990
and continues to the present, and includes Operation Iraqi Freedom
(OIF) and Operation New Dawn (OND).

Embedded Fragment Registry: OEF, OIF, and OND Veterans who
have or likely have an embedded fragment as the result of an injury
they received while serving in an area of conflict.

Agent Orange Registry: Agent Orange is an herbicide that the U.S.
military used between 1962 and 1971, during the Vietnam War to re-

move jungle that provided enemy cover. Veterans serving in Vietnam were possibly exposed to Agent Orange or its dioxin contaminant. Veterans eligible for this registry evaluation are those who served on the ground in Vietnam between Jan. 9, 1962, and May 7, 1975, regardless of the length of service; this includes Veterans who served aboard boats that operated on inland waterways ("Brown Water Navy") or who made brief visits ashore. Information is also available through VA's Special Issues Helpline at 1-800-749-8387.

Ionizing Radiation Registry: For Veterans who have received nasopharyngeal (nose and throat) radium irradiation treatments while on active duty and Veterans possibly exposed to radiation.Airborne Hazards and Open Burn Pit Registry: Unlike other registries, when Veterans complete the online Airborne Hazards and Open Burn Pit Registry self-assessment questionnaire, they are in the registry. No in-person medical evaluation is required to become registered. Veterans not already enrolled in VA health care should contact an Environmental Health Coordinator at a nearby VA facility by visiting the following link: (**http://www.publichealth.va.gov/exposures/co-ordinators.asp**) or calling 1-877-222-8387.

Vet Center Readjustment Counseling Services: VA provides readjustment counseling services, to include direct counseling, outreach, and referral, through 300 community-based Vet Centers located in all 50 states, the District of Columbia, Guam, Puerto Rico, and American Samoa. Vet Center counselors provide individual, group, marriage, and family readjustment counseling to those individuals that have served in combat zones or areas of hostilities to assist them in making a successful transition from military to civilian life; to include treatment for posttraumatic stress disorder (PTSD), and help with any other military-related problems that affect functioning within the family, work, school or other areas of everyday life. Other psycho-social services include outreach, education, medical referral, homeless Veteran services, employment, VA benefit referral, and the brokering of non-VA services.

Bereavement Counseling related to Servicemembers: Bereavement counseling is available through VA's Vet Centers to all immediate family members (including spouses, children, parents, and siblings) of Servicemembers who die while serving on active service. Vet Center bereavement services for surviving family members of Servicemembers may be accessed by calling (202) 461-6530. For additional information, contact the nearest Vet Center, listed in the back of this book, or visit **www.vetcenter.va.gov/**.

Vet Center Combat Call Center: (1-877-WAR-VETS) is an around the clock confidential call center where combat Veterans and their families can call to talk about their military experience or any other issue they are facing in their readjustment to civilian life. The staff is comprised of combat Veterans from several eras as well as family members of combat Veterans.

Home Improvements and Structural Alterations: VA provides up to $6,800 lifetime benefits for service-connected Veterans/Servicemembers and up to $2,000 lifetime benefits for nonservice-connected Veterans to make home improvements and/or structural changes necessary for the continuation of treatment or for disability access to the Veterans/Servicemembers home and essential lavatory and sanitary facilities. For application information, contact the Prosthetic Representative at the nearest VA medical center.

Special Eligibility Programs: VA provides comprehensive health care benefits, including outpatient, inpatient, pharmacy, prosthetics, medical equipment, and supplies for certain Korea and Vietnam Veterans' birth children diagnosed with spina bifida (except spina bifida occulta).

Services for Blind and Visually Impaired Veterans: Severely disabled blind Veterans may be eligible for case management services at a VA medical center and for admission to an inpatient or outpatient VA blind or vision rehabilitation program.

Mental Health Care Treatment: Veterans eligible for VA medical care may receive general and specialty mental health treatment as needed. Mental health services are available in primary care clinics (including Home Based Primary Care), general and specialty mental health outpatient clinics, inpatient mental health units, residential rehabilitation and treatment programs, specialty medical clinics, and Community Living Centers. For more information on VA mental health services, visit **http://www.mentalhealth.va.gov/VAMentalHealthGroup.asp**.

Veterans Crisis Line: Veterans experiencing emotional distress/crisis, or who need to talk to a trained mental health professional, may call the Veterans Crisis Line, 1-800-273-TALK (8255). The hotline is available 24 hours a day, seven days a week. When callers press "1," they are immediately connected with a qualified and caring provider who can help.

Chat feature: Veterans Chat is located at www.Veterancrisisline.net by clicking on the Veterans chat tab on the right side of the webpage. Text feature: Those in crisis may text 83-8255 free of charge to receive confidential, personal and immediate support. European access: Veterans and members of the military community in Europe may dial 0800-1273-8255 or DSN 118. For more information about VA's suicide prevention program, visit: **http://www.mentalhealth**. va.gov/suicide_prevention/ or **www.veteranscrisisline.net**.

The **PTSD Coach** is a mobile application that provides information about PTSD, self-assessment and symptom management tools and information about how to connect with resources that are available for those who might be dealing with post-trauma effects. The PTSD Coach is available as a free download for iPhone or Android devices.

Outpatient Dental Treatment: Dental benefits are provided by VA according to law. In some instances, VA is authorized to provide extensive dental care, while in other cases treatment may be limited by law. For more information about eligibility for VA medical and dental benefits, contact VA at 1-877-222-8387, or **www.va.gov/healthbenefits.**

Vocational and Work Assistance Programs
VHA Therapeutic & Supported Employment Services (TSES) Programs: These programs are designed to assist Veterans to live and work as independently as possible in their respective communities. Participation in TSES vocational services cannot be used to deny or discontinue VA disability benefits. Payments received from Compensated Work Therapy Sheltered Workshop and Transitional Work and Incentive Therapy cannot be used to deny or discontinue SSI and/or SSDI payments and they are not subject to IRS taxes.

Long-term Services: VA provides institution based services (nursing home level of care) to Veterans through three national programs: VA owned and operated Community Living Centers (CLC), State Veterans' Homes owned and operated by the states, and the community nursing home program. Each program has admission and eligibility criteria specific to the program. VA is obligated to pay the full cost of nursing home services for enrolled Veterans who need nursing home care for a service-connected disability, or Veterans or who have a 70 percent or greater service-connected disability and Veterans with a rating of total disability based on individual un-employability. VA provided nursing home care for all other Veterans is based on available resources.

Emergency Medical Care in U.S. Non-VA Facilities: In the case of medical emergencies, VA may reimburse or pay for emergency non-VA medical care not previously authorized that is provided to certain eligible Veterans when VA or other federal facilities are not feasibly available. This benefit may be dependent upon other conditions, such as notification to VA, the nature of treatment sought, the status of the Veteran, the presence of other health care insurance, and third party liability. Because there are different regulatory requirements that may affect VA payment and Veteran liability for the cost of care, it is very important that the nearest VA medical facility to where emergency services are furnished be notified as soon as possible after emergency treatment is sought.

Foreign Medical Program: VA may authorize reimbursement for medical services for service-connected disabilities or any disability associated with and found to be aggravating a service-connected disability for those Veterans living or traveling outside the United States. Veterans calling from within the Philippines may contact the VA office in Pasay City at 1-800-1888-8782. If calling from outside of the Philippines, the number is 011-632-318-8387. Veterans may also register by email at IRIS.va.gov. All other Veterans living or planning to travel outside the U.S. should register with the Foreign Medical Program, P.O. Box 469061, Denver, CO 80246-9061, USA; telephone 303-331-7590. For information, visit: **http://www.va.gov/hac/forbeneficiaries/fmp/fmp.asp**.

Caregiver Programs and Services: VA has long supported family caregivers as vital partners in providing care worthy of the sacrifices of America's Veterans and Servicemembers. Each VA medical center has a Caregiver Support Program coordinated by a Caregiver Support Coordinator (CSC). The CSC coordinates caregiver activities and serves as a resource expert for Veterans, their families and VA providers.

Non-health care Benefits

Disability Compensation

Disability compensation is a monetary benefit paid to Veterans who are determined by VA to be disabled by an injury or illness that was incurred or aggravated during active military service. These disabilities are considered to be service connected. To be eligible for compensation, the Veteran must have been separated or discharged under conditions other than dishonorable.

Monthly disability compensation varies with the degree of disability and the number of eligible dependents. Veterans with certain severe disabilities may be eligible for additional special monthly compensation (SMC). Disability compensation benefits are not subject to federal or state income tax. Detailed compensation rate information can be found at **http://www.benefits.va.gov/COMPENSATION/resources_comp02.asp**.

The payment of military retirement pay, disability severance pay and separation incentive payments, known as Special Separation Benefit (SSB) and Voluntary Separation Incentive (VSI), may affect the amount of VA compensation paid to disabled Veterans. For additional details on types of disability claims and how to apply, go to http://benefits.va.gov/benefits/.

Veterans with disability ratings of at least 30 percent are eligible for additional allowances for dependents, including spouses, minor

2015 VA Disability Compensation with no dependents

Disability Rating	Monthly Rate
10 percent	$133.17
20 percent	$263.23
30 percent*	$407.75
40 percent*	$587.36
50 percent*	$836.13
60 percent*	$1,059.09
70 percent*	$1,334.71
80 percent*	$1,551.48
90 percent*	$1,743.48
100 percent*	$2,906.83

2015 VA Disability Compensation with a spouse

Disability Rating	Monthly Rate
10 percent	$133.17
20 percent	$263.23
30 percent*	$455.75
40 percent*	$651.36
50 percent*	$917.13
60 percent*	$1,156.09
70 percent*	$1,447.71
80 percent*	$1,680.48
90 percent*	$1,888.48
100 percent*	$3,068.90

Detailed information about Disability Compensation is available at **http://www.benefits.va.gov/COMPENSATION/resources-rates-read-compAndSMC.asp.** *This page lists comprehensive rate information and detailed instructions on calculating benefits.*

children, children between the ages of 18 and 23 who are attending school, children who are permanently incapable of self-support because of a disability arising before age 18, and dependent parents. The additional amount depends on the disability rating and the number of dependents.

Dependency and Indemnity Compensation (DIC) is a tax free monetary benefit generally payable to a surviving spouse, child, or parent of Servicemembers who died while on active duty, active duty for training, or inactive duty training or survivors of Veterans who died from their service-connected disabilities. DIC for parents is an income based benefit. For more detailed information, visit **http://www.benefits.va.gov/COMPENSATION/types-dependency_and_indemnity_parents.asp**.

Additional Benefits for Eligible Military Retirees

Concurrent Retirement and Disability Pay (CRDP) is a DoD program that allows some individuals to receive both military retired pay and VA disability compensation. Normally, such concurrent receipt is prohibited. Veterans do not need to apply for this benefit, as payment is coordinated between VA and the military pay center. To qualify for CRDP, Veterans must have a VA service-connected rating of 50 percent or greater, be eligible to receive retired pay, and:

- Be retired from military service based on longevity, including Temporary Early Retirement Authority (TERA) retirees; or
- Be retired due to disability with 20 or more qualifying years of service*; or
- Be retired from National Guard or Reserve service with 20 or more qualifying years.

* For Veterans who retired due to disability with 20 or more qualifying years, CRDP is subject to an offset for the difference between retired pay based on disability and retired pay based on longevity.

Housing Grants for Disabled Veterans Certain Servicemembers and Veterans with service-connected disabilities may be entitled to a housing grant from VA to help build a new specially adapted house, to adapt a home they already own, or buy a house and modify it to meet their disability-related requirements. Eligible Veterans or Servicemembers may now receive up to three grants, with the total dollar amount of the grants not to exceed the maximum allowable. Previous grant recipients who had received assistance of less than the current maximum allowable may be eligible for an additional grant.

Special Home Adaption (SHA) Grant: VA may approve a benefit amount up to a maximum of $13,511 for the cost of necessary adaptations to a Servicemember's or Veteran's residence or to help him/her acquire a residence already adapted with special features for his/her disability, to purchase and adapt a home, or for adaptations to a family member's home in which they will reside.

Temporary Residence Adaptation (TRA): Eligible Veterans and Servicemembers who are temporarily residing in a home owned by a family member may also receive a TRA grant to help the Veteran or Servicemember adapt the family member's home to meet his or her special needs. Those eligible for a $67,555 grant would be permitted to use up to $29,657 and those eligible for a $13,511 grant would be permitted to use up to $5,295. Grant amounts are adjusted Oct.1 every year based on a cost-of-construction index.
For more information on SAH, visit **http://www.benefits.va.gov/ homeloans/sah.asp**.

Automobile Allowance: As of Oct. 1, 2013, Veterans and Service-members may be eligible for a one-time payment of not more than $19,817 toward the purchase of an automobile or other conveyance if they have service-connected loss or permanent loss of use of one or both hands or feet, or permanent impairment of vision of both eyes to a certain degree. To apply, contact a VA regional office at 1-800-827-1000 or the nearest VA health care facility.

Clothing Allowance: Any Veteran who has service-connected disabilities that require a prosthetic or orthopedic appliances may receive clothing allowances. This allowance is also available to any Veteran whose service-connected skin condition requires prescribed medication that irreparably damages outer garments. To apply, contact the prosthetic representative at the nearest VA medical center.

Allowance for Aid and Attendance or Housebound Veterans
A Veteran who is determined by VA to be in need of the regular aid and attendance of another person, or a Veteran who is permanently housebound, may be entitled to additional disability compensation or pension payments. A Veteran evaluated at 30 percent or more disabled is entitled to receive an additional payment for a spouse who is in need of the aid and attendance of another person.

Vocational Rehabilitation and Employment

Vocational Rehabilitation and Employment (VR&E), sometimes referred to as the Chapter 31 program, provides services to eligible Servicemembers and Veterans with service-connected disabilities to help them prepare for, obtain, and maintain suitable employment or achieve independence in daily living.

Eligibility for Veterans
A Veteran must have a VA service-connected disability rating of at least 20 percent with an employment handicap, or rated 10 percent with a serious employment handicap, and be discharged or released from military service under other than dishonorable conditions.

Eligibility for Servicemembers
Servicemembers are eligible to apply if they expect to receive an honorable discharge upon separation from active duty, obtain a rating of 20 percent or more from VA, obtain a proposed Disability Evaluation System (DES) rating of 20 percent or more from VA, or obtain a referral to a Physical Evaluation Board (PEB) through the

Integrated Disability Evaluation System (IDES).

Entitlement
A Vocational Rehabilitation Counselor (VRC) works with the Veteran

Subsistence Allowance
In some cases, Veterans participating in the VR&E program may receive a subsistence allowance while they pursue an educational or training program in preparation for a future career. The subsistence allowance is paid each month, and is based on the rate of attendance in a training program (full time, three quarter time, or half time), the number of dependents, and the type of training. If a Veteran qualifies for the Post-9/11 GI Bill he/she may be eligible to receive the Basic Allowance for Housing (BAH) rate for subsistence. Download the current subsistence allowance rates at http://www.benefits.va.gov/vocrehab/subsistence_allowance_rates.asp

VR&E Subsistence Allowance Rates

Training	Time	No dependents	One dependent	Two dependents	Each Additional dependent
Institutional*	Full-Time	$605.44	$751.00	$885.00	$64.50
	3/4-Time	$454.92	$564.07	$885.00	$49.61
	1/2-Time	$304.39	$377.14	$443.31	$33.10
Farm Co-op Apprentice OJT**	Full-Time	$529.36	$640.15	$737.77	$47.99
Extended Evaluation Services in Rehab Facility	Full-Time	$5605.44	$751.00	$885.00	$64.50
	3/4-Time	$454.92	$564.04	$661.67	$49.61
	1/2-Time	$304.39	$377.14	$443.31	$33.10
	1/4-Time	$152.17	$188.59	$221.65	$16.51
Independ. Living	Full-Time	$605.44	$751.00	$885.00	$64.50
	3/4-Time	$454.92	$564.07	$661.67	$49.61
	1/2-Time	$304.39	$377.14	$443.31	$33.10

to determine if an employment handicap exists. An employment handicap exists if a Veteran's service-connected disability impairs his/her ability to prepare for, obtain, and maintain suitable career employment. After an entitlement decision is made, the Veteran and VRC work together to develop a rehabilitation plan. The rehabilitation plan outlines the rehabilitation services to be provided.

Services
Based on their individualized needs, Veterans work with a VRC to select one of five tracks to employment. The Five Tracks to Employment provide greater emphasis on exploring employment options early in the rehabilitation planning process, greater informed choice for the Veteran regarding occupational and employment options, faster access to employment for Veterans who have identifiable and transferable skills for direct placement into suitable employment, and an option for Veterans who are not able to work, but need assistance to lead a more independent life. If a program of training is selected, VA pays the cost of the approved training and services (except those coordinated through other providers) that are included in an individual's rehabilitation plan, including subsistence allowance.

The Five Tracks to Employment are: reemployment with previous employer, rapid access to employment, self-employment, employment through long-term services and independent living services.

Length of a Rehabilitation Program
The basic period of eligibility in which VR&E benefits may be used is 12 years from the later of the following: 1) A Veteran's date of separation from active military service, or 2) The date VA first notified a Veteran that he/she has a compensable service-connected disability. Depending on the length of program needed, Veterans may be provided up to 48 months of full-time services or the part-time equivalent. Rehabilitation plans that only provide services to improve independence in daily living are limited to 30 months. These limitations may be extended in certain circumstances.

Employment Services
VR&E has partnerships with federal, state and private agencies to provide direct placement of Veterans or Servicemembers. VR&E can assist with placement using the following resources:

On the Job Training (OJT) Program
Employers hire Veterans at an apprentice wage, and VR&E supple-

ments the salary up the journeyman wage (up to maximum allowable under OJT). As the Veterans progress through training, the employers begin to pay more of the salary until the Veterans reach journeyman level and the employers are paying the entire salary. VR&E will also pay for any necessary tools.

Non-Paid Work Experience (NPWE)

The NPWE program provides eligible Veterans the opportunity to obtain training and practical job experience concurrently. This program is ideal for Veterans or Servicemembers who have a clearly established career goal, and who learn easily in a hands-on environment. This program is also well suited for Veterans who are having difficulties obtaining employment due to lack of work experience. The NPWE program may be established in a federal, state, or local (i.e. city, town, school district) government agencies only. The employer may hire the Veteran at any point during the NPWE.

Special Employer Incentive (SEI)

The SEI program is for eligible Veterans who face challenges in obtaining employment. Veterans approved to participate in the SEI program are hired by participating employers and employment is expected to continue following successful completion of the program. Employers may be provided this incentive to hire Veterans. If approved, the employer will receive reimbursement for up to 50 percent of the Veteran's salary during the SEI program, which can last up to six months.

The Veterans Employment Center (www.ebenefits.va.gov/ebenefits/jobs) is the federal government's single authoritative online source for connecting transitioning Servicemembers, Veterans, and military families with meaningful career opportunities with both public and private-sector employers.

VetSuccess On Campus (VSOC)

The VSOC program is designed to assist Veterans as they make the transition to college life. Through the VSOC program, VR&E is strengthening partnerships with institutions of higher learning and creating opportunities to help Veterans achieve success by providing outreach and transition services to the general Veteran population during their transition from military to college life.

Additional information on VR&E benefits is available at **www.benefits.va.gov/vocrehab**.

VA Pensions

Eligibility for Veterans Pension
Low-income wartime Veterans may qualify for pension if they meet
certain service, income and net worth limits set by law, are age 65 or
older, or permanently and totally disabled, or a patient in a nursing
home receiving skilled nursing care, or receiving Social Security Disability Insurance, or receiving Supplemental Security Income. Generally, a Veteran must have at least 90 days of active duty service, with
at least one day during a VA recognized wartime period. The 90-day
active service requirement does not apply to Veterans discharged
from the military due to a service-connected disability.

Note: Veterans may have to meet longer minimum periods of active
duty if they entered active duty on or after Sept. 8, 1980, or, if they
were officers who entered active duty on or after Oct. 16,1981. The
Veteran's discharge must have been under conditions other than
dishonorable and the disability must be for reasons other than the
Veteran's own willful misconduct.

Payments are made to bring the Veteran's total income, including other retirement or Social Security income, to a level set by
Congress. Unreimbursed medical expenses may reduce countable
income for VA purposes.

Protected Pension
Pension beneficiaries, who were receiving a VA pension on Dec. 31,
1978, and do not wish to elect the Improved Pension, will continue
to receive the pension rate received on that date. This rate generally
continues as long as the beneficiary's income remains within established limits, or net worth does not bar payment, and the beneficiary
does not lose any dependents.

Beneficiaries must continue to meet basic eligibility factors, such as
permanent and total disability for Veterans. VA must adjust rates for
other reasons, such as a Veteran's hospitalization in a VA facility.

Veterans Pension
Congress establishes the maximum annual Veterans Pension rates.
Payments are reduced by the amount of countable income of the
Veteran, spouse, and dependent children. When a Veteran without
a spouse or a child is furnished nursing home or domiciliary care

by VA, the pension is reduced to an amount not to exceed $90 per month after three calendar months of care. The reduction may be delayed if nursing-home care is being continued to provide the Veteran with rehabilitation services.

Aid and Attendance and Housebound Benefits
(Special Monthly Pension)

Veterans and surviving spouses who are eligible for VA pensions are eligible for higher maximum pension rates if they qualify for aid and attendance or housebound benefits. An eligible individual may qualify if he or she requires the regular aid of another person in order to perform personal functions required in everyday living, or is bedridden, a patient in a nursing home due to mental or physical incapacity, blind, or permanently and substantially confined to his/her immediate premises because of a disability. Claimants may apply for aid and attendance or housebound benefits by completing VA Form 21-2680 (available through **www.va.gov**). Claimants may also write to the nearest VA regional office and include copies of any evidence, preferably a report from an attending physician or a nursing home, validating the need for aid and attendance or housebound care. VA also pays a special $90 monthly rate to pension-eligible Veterans or surviving spouses with no dependents who receive Medicaid-covered nursing home care. These funds are available for the beneficiary's personal use and may not be used to offset the cost of his or her care.

Education and Training

Additional information can be found at **www.benefits.va.gov/gibill/** or by calling 1-888-GI-BILL-1 (1-888-442-4551).

Post–9/11 GI Bill

Eligibility

The Post-9/11 GI Bill is an education benefit program for Servicemembers and Veterans who served on active duty after Sept.10, 2001. Benefits are payable for training pursued on or after Aug. 1, 2009. No payments can be made under this program for training pursued before that date.

To be eligible, the Servicemember or Veteran must serve at least 90 aggregate days on active duty after Sept. 10, 2001, and remain on active duty or be honorably discharged. Active duty includes active service performed by National Guard members under title 32 U.S.C. for the purposes of organizing, administering, recruiting, instructing, or training the National Guard; or under section 502(f) for the purpose of responding to a national emergency. Veterans may also be eligible if they were honorably discharged from active duty for a service-connected disability after serving 30 continuous days after Sept. 10, 2001. Generally, Servicemembers or Veterans may receive up to 36 months of entitlement under the Post-9/11 GI Bill.

Eligibility for benefits expires 15 years from the last period of active duty of at least 90 consecutive days. If released for a service-connected disability after at least 30 days of continuous service, eligibility ends 15 years from when the member is released for the service-connected disability.

If, on Aug. 1, 2009, the Servicemember or Veteran is eligible for the Montgomery GI Bill; the Montgomery GI Bill – Selected Reserve; or the Reserve Educational Assistance Program, and qualifies for the Post-9/11 GI Bill, an irrevocable election must be made to receive benefits under the Post-9/11 GI Bill. In most instances, once the election to receive benefits under the Post-9/11 GI Bill is made, the individual will no longer be eligible to receive benefits under the relinquished program. Based on the length of active duty service, eligible participants are entitled to receive a percentage of the following:

- Cost of in-state tuition and fees at public institutions and for the 2013-2014 academic year, up to $19,198.31 toward tuition and fee costs at private and foreign institutions (paid directly to the school),
- Monthly housing allowance* equal to the basic allowance for housing payable to a military E-5 with dependents, in the same ZIP code as the primary school (paid directly to the Servicemember, Veteran, or eligible dependents),
- Yearly books and supplies stipend of up to $1,000 per year (paid directly to the Servicemember, Veteran, or eligible dependents), and
- A one-time payment of $500 paid to certain individuals relocating from highly rural areas.

Housing allowance is not payable to individuals pursuing training at half time or less.

Approved training under the Post-9/11 GI Bill includes graduate and undergraduate degrees, vocational/technical training, on-the-job training, flight training, correspondence training, licensing and national testing programs, and tutorial assistance.

Individuals serving an aggregate period of active duty after Sept. 10, 2001, can receive the following percentages based on length of service:

Individuals serving an aggregate period of active duty after Sept. 10, 2001, can receive the percentages listed in the chart on page 54 based on length of service:
1. Includes service on active duty in entry level and skill training.
2. Excludes service on active duty in entry level and skill training.
3. If the individual would only qualify at the 70 percent level when service on active duty in entry level and skill training is excluded, then VA can only pay at the 70 percent level.

The Yellow Ribbon G.I. Bill Education Enhancement Program
This program may assist eligible individuals with payment of their tuition and fees in instances where costs exceed the in-state tuition charges at a public institution or the national maximum payable at private and foreign institutions. To be eligible, the student must be: a Veteran receiving benefits at the 100-percent benefit rate payable, a transfer-of-entitlement-eligible dependent child, or a transfer-of-entitlement-eligible spouse of a Veteran.

Marine Gunnery Sergeant John David Fry Scholarship
This scholarship entitles children of those who die in the line of duty on or after Sept. 11, 2001, to use Post-9/11 GI Bill benefits.

Eligible children:
- Are entitled to 36 months of benefits at the 100 percent level,
- Have 15 years to use the benefit beginning on their 18th birthday,
- May use the benefit until their 33rd birthday, and
- Are not eligible for the Yellow Ribbon Program.

VetSuccess on Campus
This is designed to provide on-campus benefits assistance and re-adjustment counseling to assist Veterans in completing their college educations and entering the labor market in viable careers. Under

this program, a full-time, experienced Vocational Rehabilitation Counselor and a part-time Vet Center Outreach Coordinator are assigned at each campus to provide VA benefits outreach, support, and assistance to ensure their health, educational, and benefit needs are met.

Montgomery GI Bill

Eligibility
VA educational benefits may be used while the Servicemember is on active duty or after the Servicemember's separation from active duty with a fully honorable military discharge. Discharges "under honorable conditions" and "general" discharges do not establish eligibility. Eligibility generally expires 10 years after the Servicemember's discharge. However, there are exceptions for disability, re-entering active duty, and upgraded discharges. All participants must have a high school diploma, equivalency certificate, or have completed 12 hours toward a college degree before applying for benefits.

Home Loan Guaranty

VA home loan guaranties are issued to help eligible Servicemembers, Veterans, Reservists, National Guard members, and certain surviving spouses obtain homes, condominiums, and manufactured homes, and to refinance loans. For additional information or to obtain VA loan guaranty forms, visit **http://www.benefits.va.gov/homeloans/**.

Eligibility
In addition to the periods of eligibility and conditions of service requirements, applicants must have a good credit rating, sufficient income, a valid Certificate of Eligibility (COE), and agree to live in the property in order to be approved by a lender for a VA home loan. Lenders can apply for a COE online through the Veterans Information Portal (https:// vip.vba.va.gov/portal/VBAH/Home). Active duty Servicemembers and Veterans can also apply online at **http://www.ebenefits.va.gov**. Although it's preferable to apply electronically, it is possible to apply for a COE using VA Form 26-1880, Request for Certificate of Eligibility.

In applying for a hard-copy COE from VA Eligibility Center using VA Form 26-1880, it is typically necessary that the eligible Veteran present a copy of his/her report of discharge or DD Form 214, Certificate of Release or Discharge from Active Duty, or other adequate substitute evidence to VA. An eligible active duty Servicemember should obtain and submit a statement of service signed by an appropriate military official to the VA Eligibility Center. A completed VA Form 26-1880 and any associated documentation should be mailed to Atlanta Regional Loan Center, Attn: COE (262), P.O. Box 100034, Decatur, GA 30031. Please note that while VA's electronic applications can establish eligibility and issue an online COE in a matter of seconds, not all cases can be processed online.

Surviving Spouses: Some spouses of Veterans may have home loan eligibility. They are:

- the unmarried surviving spouse of a Veteran who died as a result of service or service-connected causes,
- the surviving spouse of a Veteran who dies on active duty or from service-connected causes, who remarries on or after attaining age 57 and on or after Dec. 16, 2003, and
- the spouse of an active duty member who is listed as missing in action (MIA) or a prisoner of war (POW) for at least 90 days.

VA Appraisals

No loan can be guaranteed by VA without first being appraised by a VA-assigned fee appraiser. A lender can request a VA appraisal through VA systems. The Veteran borrower typically pays for the appraisal upon completion, according to a fee schedule approved by VA. This VA appraisal estimates value of the property. It is not an inspection and does not guarantee the house is free of defects.

Closing Costs

For purchase home loans, payment in cash is required on all closing costs, including title search and recording fees, hazard insurance premiums and prepaid taxes. For refinancing loans, all such costs may be included in the loan, as long as the total loan does not exceed the reasonable value of the property. Interest rate reduction loans may include closing costs, including a maximum of two discount points.

VA Funding Fees

A funding fee must be paid to VA unless the Veteran is exempt from such a fee. The fee may be paid in cash or included in the loan. Closing costs such as VA appraisal, credit report, loan processing fee, title search, title insurance, recording fees, transfer taxes, survey charges, or hazard insurance may not be included for purchase home loans.

All Veterans, except those who are specified by law as exempt, are charged a VA funding fee. For all types of loans, the loan amount may include this funding fee.

VA funding fee and up to $6,000 of energy-efficient improvements can be included in VA loans. However, no other fees, charges, or discount points may be included in the loan amount for regular purchase or construction loans. For refinancing loans, most closing costs may be included in the loan amount.

Required Occupancy
To qualify for a VA home loan, a Veteran or the spouse of an active-duty Servicemember must certify that he or she intends to occupy the home. A dependent child of an active-duty Servicemember also satisfies the occupancy requirement.

Financing, Interest Rates and Terms
Veterans obtain VA-guaranteed loans through the usual lending institutions, including banks, credit unions, and mortgage brokers. VA-guaranteed loans can have either a fixed interest rate or an adjustable rate, where the interest rate may adjust up to one percent annually and up to five percent over the life of the loan. VA does not set the interest rate. Interest rates are negotiable between the lender and borrower on all loan types.

Loan Assumption Requirements and Liability
VA loans made on or after March 1, 1988, are not assumable without the prior approval of VA or its authorized agent (usually the lender collecting the monthly payments). To approve the assumption, the lender must ensure that the purchaser is a satisfactory credit risk and will assume all of the Veteran's liabilities on the loan. If approved, the purchaser will have to pay a funding fee that the lender sends to VA, and the Veteran will be released from liability to the federal government.

Loans made prior to Mar. 1, 1988, are generally freely assumable, but Veterans should still request the lender's approval in order to be released of liability. Veterans whose loans were closed after Dec. 31, 1989, usually have no liability to the government following a foreclosure, except in cases involving fraud, misrepresentation, or bad faith, such as allowing an unapproved assumption. However, for the entitlement to be restored, any loss suffered by VA must be paid in full.

VA Assistance to Veterans in Default

VA urges all Veterans who are encountering problems making their mortgage payments to speak with their servicers as soon as possible to explore options to avoid foreclosure. Contrary to popular opinion, servicers do not want to foreclose because foreclosure costs money. Depending on a Veteran's specific situation, servicers may offer any of the following options to avoid foreclosure:

- Repayment Plan – The borrower makes a regular installment each month plus part of the missed installments.
- Special Forbearance – The servicer agrees not to initiate foreclosure to allow time for borrowers to repay the missed installments. An example of when this would be likely is when a borrower is waiting for a tax refund.
- Loan Modification– Provides the borrower a fresh start by adding the delinquency to the loan balance and establishing a new payment schedule.
- Additional time to arrange a private sale – The servicer agrees to delay foreclosure to allow a sale to close if the loan will be paid.
- Short Sale – When the servicer agrees to allow a borrower to sell his/her home for a lesser amount than what is currently required to pay off the loan.
- Deed-in-Lieu of Foreclosure – The borrower voluntarily agrees to deed the property to the servicer instead of going through a lengthy foreclosure process.

Servicemembers Civil Relief Act

Veteran borrowers may be able to request relief pursuant to the Servicemembers Civil Relief Act (SCRA). In order to qualify for certain protections available under the Act, their obligation must have originated prior to their current period of active military service. SCRA may provide a lower interest rate during military service and for up to one year after service ends, provide forbearance, or prevent foreclosure or eviction up to nine months from period of military service.

Assistance to Veterans with VA-Guaranteed Home Loans

When a VA-guaranteed home loan becomes delinquent, VA may provide supplemental servicing assistance to help cure the default. The servicer has the primary responsibility of servicing the loan to resolve the default. Veterans with VA-guaranteed home loans can call 1-877-

827-3702 to reach the nearest VA office where loan specialists are prepared to discuss potential ways to help save the loan.

Preventing Veteran Homelessness
Veterans who feel they may be facing homelessness as a result of losing their home can call 1-877-4AID VET (877-424-3838) or go to **http://www.va.gov/HOMELESS/index.asp** to receive assistance from VA.

Assistance to Veterans with Non-VA Guaranteed Home Loans
For Veterans or Servicemembers who have a non-VA-guaranteed or sub-prime loan, VA has a network of eight Regional Loan Centers and a special servicing centers in Hawaii that can offer advice and guidance. Borrowers may visit **www.benefits.va.gov/homeloans/**, or call toll free -1-877-827-3702 to speak with a VA loan technician. However, unlike when a Veteran has a VA-guaranteed home loan, VA does not have the authority to intervene on the borrower's behalf.

VA Refinancing of a Non-VA Guaranteed Home Loan
Veterans with non-VA guaranteed home loans now have new options for refinancing to a VA-guaranteed home loan. These new options are available as a result of the Veterans' Benefits Improvement Act of 2008. Veterans who wish to refinance their subprime or conventional mortgage may now do so for up to 100 percent of value of the property.

Other Assistance for Delinquent Veteran Borrowers
If VA is not able to help a Veteran borrower retain his/her home (whether a VA-guaranteed loan or not), the Department of Housing and Urban Development (HUD) offers assistance to homeowners by sponsoring local housing counseling agencies. To find an approved agency in your area, please search online at **http://www.hud.gov/ offices/hsg/sfh/hcc/hcs.cfm**, or call HUD's interactive voice system at (800) 569-4287.

VA Life Insurance

For complete details on government life insurance, visit **www.benefits.va.gov/insurance/** or call VA's Insurance Center toll-free at 1-800-669-8477. Specialists are available between the hours of 8:30 a.m. and 6 p.m., Eastern Time, to discuss premium payments, insurance dividends, address changes, policy loans, naming beneficiaries, reporting the death of the insured, and other insurance issues.

If the insurance policy number is not known, provide whatever information is available, such as the Veteran's VA file number, date of birth, Social Security number, military serial number or military service branch and dates of service. To provide the information by mail, send it to:

Department of Veterans Affairs
Insurance Center
PO Box 42954
Philadelphia, PA 19101

For information about Servicemembers' Group Life Insurance, Veterans' Group Life Insurance, Servicemembers' Group Life Insurance Traumatic Injury Protection, or Servicemembers' Group Life Insurance Family Coverage, visit the Website above or call the Office of Servicemembers' Group Life Insurance directly at 1-800-419-1473.

Servicemembers' Group Life Insurance (SGLI)
The following are automatically insured for $400,000 under SGLI:

1. Active duty members of the Army, Navy, Air Force, Marines and Coast Guard.
2. Commissioned members of the National Oceanic and Atmospheric Administration (NOAA) and the Public Health Service (PHS).
3. Cadets or midshipmen of the U.S. military academies.
4. Members, cadets and midshipmen of the ROTC while engaged in authorized training and practice cruises.
5. Members of the Ready Reserves/National Guard who are scheduled to perform at least 12 periods of inactive training per year.
6. Members who volunteer for a mobilization category in the Individual Ready Reserve.

Individuals may elect in writing to be covered for a lesser amount or to decline coverage. SGLI coverage is available in $50,000 increments up to the maximum of $400,000.

Full-time Servicemembers on active duty are covered 24/7, 365 days of the year. Coverage is in effect during the period of active duty or inactive duty training and for 120 days following separation or release from duty. Reservists or National Guard members who have been assigned to a unit in which they are scheduled to perform at least 12 periods of inactive duty that is creditable for retirement purposes are also covered 24/7, 365 days of the year and for 120 days following separation or release from duty.

Part-time coverage is provided for Reservists or National Guard members who do not qualify for the full-time coverage described above. Part-time coverage generally applies to Reservists/National Guard members who drill only a few days in a year. These individuals are covered only while on active duty or active duty for training, or traveling to and from such duty. Members covered part-time do not receive 120 days of free coverage after separation unless they incur or aggravate a disability during a period of duty

SGLI Traumatic Injury Protection (TSGLI)
Members of the armed services serve our nation heroically during times of great need, but what happens when they experience great needs of their own because they have sustained a traumatic injury? TSGLI provides for payment traumatically injured Servicemembers who have suffered certain physical losses. The TSGLI benefit ranges between $25,000 and $100,000 depending on the loss,. TSGLI helps Servicemembers by allowing their families to be with them during their recovery or by helping with other expenses incurred during their recovery period.

TSGLI is attached to SGLI. An additional $1.00 is added to the Servicemember's SGLI premium to cover TSGLI. After Dec. 1, 2005, all Servicemembers who are covered by SGLI are automatically also covered by TSGLI. TSGLI cannot be declined unless the Servicemember also declines basic SGLI. TSGLI claims are adjudicated by the individual military branches of service. In addition, there is retroactive TSGLI coverage for Servicemembers who sustained a qualifying loss between Oct. 7, 2001, and Nov. 30, 2005, regardless of where it occurred TSGLI coverage is payable to these Servicemembers regardless of whether they had SGLI coverage in force at the time of their injury.

For more information and branch of service contact information, visit

http://benefits.va.gov/insurance/tsgli.asp, or call 1-800-237-1336 (Army); 1-800-368-3202 (Navy); 1-877-216-0825 (Marine Corps); 1-800-433-0048 (Active Duty Air Force); 1-800-525-0102 (Air Force Reserves); 1-240-612-9140 (Air National Guard); 1-703-872-6647 (U.S. Coast Guard); 1-301-427-3280 (PHS); or 1-301-713-3444 (NOAA).

Servicemembers' Group Life Insurance Family Coverage (FSGLI): coverage consists of spousal coverage and dependent child coverage. FSGLI provides up to $100,000 of life insurance coverage for spouses of Servicemembers with full-time SGLI coverage, not to exceed the amount of SGLI the member has in force. Premiums for spouse coverage are based on the age of the spouse and the amount of FSGLI coverage. FSGLI is a Servicemembers' benefit; the member pays the premium and is the only person allowed to be the beneficiary of the coverage. FSGLI spousal coverage ends 120 days after any of the following events: 1) the Servicemember elects in writing to terminate coverage on the spouse; 2) the Servicemember elects to terminate his or her own SGLI coverage; 3) the Servicemember dies; 4) the Servicemember separates from service; or 5) the Servicemember is divorced from the spouse. The insured spouse may convert his or her FSGLI coverage to a permanent policy offered by participating private insurers within 120 days of the date of any of the termination events noted above. FSGLI dependent coverage of $10,000 is also automatically provided for dependent children of Servicemembers insured under SGLI, with no premium required.

Veterans' Group Life Insurance (VGLI)

SGLI may be converted to VGLI, which provides renewable term coverage to:
1. Veterans who had full-time SGLI coverage upon separation from active duty or the Reserves.
2. Members of the Ready Reserves/National Guard with part-time SGLI coverage who incur a disability or aggravate a pre-existing disability during a period of active duty or a period of inactive duty for less than 31 days that renders them uninsurable at standard premium rates.
3. Members of the Individual Ready Reserve and Inactive National Guard.

Servicemembers must apply for VGLI within one year and 120 days from separation. Servicemembers discharged on or after November 1,

2012, who apply for VGLI within 240 days of separation do not need to submit evidence of good health, while Servicemembers who apply after the 240-day period must submit evidence of insurability. The initial VGLI coverage available is equal to the amount of SGLI coverage at the time of separation from service.

Effective April 11, 2011, VGLI insureds who are under age 60 and have less than $400,000 in coverage can purchase up to $25,000 of additional coverage on each five-year anniversary of their coverage, up to the maximum $400,000. No medical underwriting is required for the additional coverage.

SGLI Disability Extension
Servicemembers who are totally disabled at the time of separation (unable to work or have certain statutory conditions), can apply for the SGLI Disability Extension, which provides free coverage for up to two years from the date of separation. To apply, Servicmembers must complete and return SGLV 8715, the SGLI Disability Extension Application.

Those covered under the SGLI Disability Extension are automatically converted to VGLI at the end of their extension period, subject to the payment of premiums. VGLI is convertible at any time to a permanent plan policy with any participating commercial insurance company.

Accelerated Death Benefits
Like many private life insurance companies, the SGLI, FSGLI and VGLI programs offer an accelerated benefits option to terminally ill insured members. An insured member is considered to be terminally ill if he or she has a written medical prognosis of nine months or less to live. All terminally ill members are eligible to receive up to 50 percent of their SGLI or VGLI coverage, and terminally ill spouses can receive up to 50 percent of their FSGLI, in a lump sum. Payment of an accelerated benefit reduces the amount payable to the beneficiaries at the time of the insured's death. To apply, an insured member must submit SGLV 8284, Servicemember/Veteran Accelerated Benefit Option Form, and spouses must complete SGLV 8284A, Servicemember Family Coverage Accelerated Benefits Option Form.

Service-Disabled Veterans' Insurance (S-DVI)
Veterans who separated from service on or after Apr. 25, 1951, un-

der other than dishonorable conditions who have service-connected disabilities, even zero percent, but are otherwise in good health, may apply to VA for up to $10,000 in life insurance coverage under the S-DVI program. Applications must be submitted within two years from the date of being notified of the approval of a new service-connected disability by VA. Veterans who are totally disabled may apply for a waiver of premiums. If approved for waiver of premiums, the Veteran can apply for additional supplemental insurance coverage of up to $30,000. However, premiums cannot be waived on the additional supplemental insurance. To be eligible for this type of supplemental insurance, Veterans must meet all of the following three requirements:

1.   Be under age 65.
2.   Be eligible for a waiver of premiums due to total disability.
3.   Apply for additional insurance within one year from the date of notification of waiver approval on the basic S-DVI policy.

Veterans' Mortgage Life Insurance (VMLI)
VMLI is mortgage protection insurance available to severely disabled Veterans who have been approved by VA for a Specially Adapted Housing (SAH) Grant. Maximum coverage is the smaller of the existing mortgage balance or $200,000, and is payable only to the mortgage company. Protection is issued automatically following SAH approval, provided the Veteran submits mortgage information required to establish a premium and does not decline coverage. Coverage automatically terminates when the mortgage is paid off. If a mortgage is disposed of through sale of the property, VMLI may be obtained on the mortgage of another home.
Other Insurance Information
The following information applies only to policies issued to World War II, Korean-era, and Vietnam-era Veterans and any Service-Disabled Veterans' Insurance policies. Policies in this group are prefixed by the letters K, V, RS, W, J, JR, JS, or RH.

Insurance Dividends Issued Annually: World War II and Korean-era Veterans with active policies beginning with the letters V, RS, W, J, JR, JS, or K earn tax-free dividends annually on the policy anniversary date. (Policies prefixed by RH do not earn dividends.) Policyholders do not need to apply for dividends, but may select from among the following dividend options:
   1. Cash: The dividend is paid directly to the insured by direct

deposit to a bank account or by check.
2. **Paid-Up Additional Insurance:** The dividend is used to purchase additional insurance coverage.
3. **Credit or Deposit:** The dividend is held in an account for the policyholder with interest. Withdrawals from the account can be made at any time. The interest rate may be adjusted.
4. **Net Premium Billing Options:** These options use the dividend to pay the annual policy premium. If the dividend exceeds the premium, the policyholder has options to choose how the remainder is used. If the dividend is not enough to pay an annual premium, the policyholder is billed the balance.
5. **Other Dividend Options:** Dividends can also be used to repay a loan or pay premiums in advance.

Reinstating Lapsed Insurance
Lapsed term policies may be reinstated within five years from the date of lapse. A five-year term policy that is not lapsed at the end of the term is automatically renewed for an additional five years. Lapsed permanent plans may be reinstated within certain time limits and with certain health requirements. Reinstated permanent plan policies require repayment of all back premiums, plus interest.

Converting Term Policies
Term policies are renewed automatically every five years, with premiums increasing at each renewal. Premiums do not increase after age 70. Term policies may be converted to permanent plans, which have fixed premiums for life and earn cash and loan values.
ividends on Capped Term Policies
Effective Sept. 2000, VA provides either a cash dividend or paid-up insurance on term policies whose premiums have been capped. Veterans with National Service Life Insurance (NSLI) term insurance that has renewed at age 71 or older and who stop paying premiums on their policies will be given a "termination dividend." This dividend can either be received as a cash payment or used to purchase a reduced amount of paid-up insurance, which insures the Veteran for life with no premium payments required. The amount of the reduced paid-up insurance remains level. This does not apply to S-DVI (RH) policies.

Borrowing on Policies
Policyholders with permanent plan policies may borrow up to 94 percent of the cash surrender value of their insurance after the insur-

ance is in force for one year or more. Interest is compounded annually. The loan interest rate is variable and may be obtained by calling toll-free 1-800-669-8477.

Reserve and National Guard

Re-employment Rights
A person who left a civilian job to enter active duty in the armed forces is entitled to return to the job after discharge or release from active duty if they:
1. Gave advance notice of military service to the employer.
2. Did not exceed five years cumulative absence from the civilian job (with some exceptions).
3. Submitted a timely application for re-employment.
4. Did not receive a dishonorable or other punitive discharge.

The law calls for a returning Veteran to be placed in the job as if he/she had never left, including benefits based on seniority such as pensions, pay increases and promotions. The law also prohibits discrimination in hiring, promotion, or other advantages of employment on the basis of military service. Veterans seeking re-employment should apply, verbally or in writing, to the company's hiring official and keep a record of their application. If problems arise, contact the Department of Labor's Veterans' Employment and Training Service (VETS) in the state of the employer.

Federal employees not properly re-employed may appeal directly to the Merit Systems Protection Board. Non-federal employees may file complaints in U.S. District Court. For information, visit **www.dol.gov/vets/programs/userra/main.htm**.

Special Groups of Veterans

Veterans Needing Fiduciary Services
The fiduciary program provides oversight of VA's most vulnerable beneficiaries who are unable to manage their VA benefits because of injury, disease, the infirmities of advanced age, or being under 18 years of age. VA appoints fiduciaries who manage VA benefits for these beneficiaries and conducts oversight of VA-appointed fiducia-

ries to ensure that they are meeting the needs of the beneficiaries they serve.

VA closely monitors fiduciaries for compliance with program responsibilities to ensure that VA benefits are being used for the purpose of meeting the needs, security, and comfort of beneficiaries and their dependents. In deciding who should act as fiduciary for a beneficiary, VA will always select the most effective and least restrictive fiduciary arrangement. For more information about VA's fiduciary program, please visit our website at http://benefits.va.gov/fiduciary/index.asp.

Homeless Veterans
VA's **homeless programs** constitute the largest integrated network of homeless assistance programs in the country, offering a wide array of services to help Veterans recover from homelessness and live as self-sufficiently and independently as possible.

VA **Health Care for Homeless Veterans** (HCHV) Program provides a gateway to VA and community supportive services for eligible Veterans. Through the HCHV Program, Veterans are provided with case management and residential treatment in the community. The program also conducts outreach to homeless Veterans who are not likely to come to VA facilities on their own.

Homeless Veterans Supported Employment Program (HVSEP) provides vocational assistance, job development and placement, and ongoing employment supports designed to improve employment outcomes among homeless Veterans. HVSEP is coordinated between CWT and the continuum of Homeless Veterans Programs for the purpose of providing community-based vocational and employment services. For more information, please visit: **http://www.va.gov/ homeless/employment_programs.asp**.

VA's **Homeless Providers Grant and Per Diem Program** provides funds to non-profit community agencies providing transitional housing (up to 24 months) and/or offering services to homeless Veterans, such as case management, education, crisis intervention, counseling, and services targeted towards specialized populations including homeless women Veterans. The goal of the program is to help homeless Veterans achieve residential stability, increase their skill levels and/or income, and obtain greater self-determination. For more information, please visit: **http://www.va.gov/homeless/gpd.asp**.

The Housing and Urban Development-Veterans Affairs Supportive Housing (HUD-VASH) Program provides permanent housing aand case management for eligible homeless Veterans who need community-based support to keep stable housing. This program allows eligible Veterans to live in Veteran-selected housing units with a "Housing Choice" voucher. These vouchers are portable to support the Veteran's choice of housing in communities served by their VA medical facility where case management services can be provided. For more information, please visit: **http//www.va.gov/homeless/ hud-vash.asp**.

The **Supportive Services for Veterans Families** (SSVF) Program is designed to rapidly re-house homeless Veteran families and prevent homelessness for those at imminent risk due to a housing crisis. Funds are granted to private non-profit organizations and consumer cooperatives that will assist very low-income Veteran families by providing a range of supportive services designed to promote housing stability. Tolocate a SSVF provider in your community, please visit **http://www.va.gov/homeless/ssvf.asp** and look for the list of current year SSVF providers or call VA's National call Center for Homeless Veterans at 1-888-4AIDVET (1-888-424-3838).

The **Veterans Justice Outreach Program** (VJO) offers outreach and case management to Veteran involved in law enforcement encounters, overseen by treatment courts, and incarcerated in local jails who may be at risk for homelessness upon their release.

The **Health Care for Re-Entry Veterans** (HCRV) Program offers outreach, referrals, and short-term case management assistance for incarcerated Veterans who may be at risk for homelessness upon their release. Visit **www.va.gov/homeless/** to locate an outreach worker

For more information on VA homeless programs and services, Veterans currently enrolled in VA health care can speak with their VA mental health or health care provider. Other Veterans and interested parties can find a complete list of VA health care facilities at www. va.gov, or they can call VA's general information hotline at 1-800-827-1000. If assistance is needed when contacting a VA facility, ask to speak to the Health Care for Homeless Veterans Program or the Mental Health service manager. Information is also available on VA Homeless program website at **www.va.gov/homeless**.

Filipino Veterans
World War II era Filipino Veterans are eligible for certain VA benefits. Generally, Old Philippine Scouts are eligible for VA benefits in the same manner as U.S. Veterans. Commonwealth Army Veterans, including certain organized Filipino guerrilla forces and New Philippine Scouts residing in the United States who are citizens or lawfully admitted for permanent residence, are also eligible for VA health care in the United States on the same basis as U.S. Veterans.

Certain Commonwealth Army Veterans and new Philippine Scouts may be eligible for disability compensation and burial benefits. Other Veterans of recognized guerrilla groups also may be eligible for certain VA benefits. Survivors of World War II era Filipino Veterans may be eligible for dependency and indemnity compensation. Eligibility and the rates of benefits vary based on the recipient's citizenship and place of residence. Call 1-800-827-1000 for additional information.

VA Benefits for Veterans Living Overseas
VA monetary benefits, including disability compensation, pension, educational benefits, and burial allowances, are generally payable overseas. Some programs are restricted. Home loan guaranties are available only in the United States and selected U.S. territories and possessions. Educational benefits are limited to approved, degree-granting programs in institutions of higher learning. Beneficiaries living in foreign countries should contact the nearest American embassy or consulate for help. In Canada, contact an office of Veterans Affairs Canada. For information, visit **http://www.vba.va.gov/bln/21/ Foreign/index.htm**.

Incarcerated Veterans
VA benefits are affected if a beneficiary is convicted of a felony and imprisoned for more than 60 days. Disability or death pension paid to an incarcerated beneficiary must be discontinued. Disability compensation paid to an incarcerated Veteran rated 20 percent or more disabled is limited to the 10 percent rate. For a Veteran whose disability rating is 10 percent, the payment is reduced to half of the rate payable to a Veteran evaluated as 10 percent disabled.

Any amounts not paid to the Veteran while incarcerated may be apportioned to eligible dependents. Payments are not reduced for participants in work-release programs, residing in halfway houses, or under community control. Failure to notify VA of a Veteran's incarceration can result in overpayment of benefits and the subsequent loss of all VA financial benefits until the overpayment is recovered. VA benefits will not be provided to any Veteran or dependent wanted for an outstanding felony warrant.

The **Health Care for Reentry Veterans Program (HCRV)** offers outreach to Veterans incarcerated in state and federal prisons, and referrals and short-term case management assistance upon release from prison. he Veterans Justice Outreach Program (VJO) offers outreach and case management to Veterans involved in law enforcement encounters, overseen by treatment courts, and incarcerated in local jails. Visit **www.va.gov/homeless/** to locate an outreach worker.

The **Veterans Justice Outreach (VJO)** Program offers outreach and linkage to needed treatment and services to Veterans involved in law enforcement encounters, seen in the court system, and/or incarcerated in local jails who may be at risk for homelessness upon their release. Visit **http://www.va.gov/HOMELESS/VJO.asp** to locate a Veterans Justice Outreach Specialist.

The Health Care for Re-Entry Veterans (HCRV) Program offers outreach, linkage to needed treatment and services, and short-term case management assistance for Veterans incarcerated in state or federal prison who may be at risk for homelessness upon their release. Visit **http://www.va.gov/HOMELESS/Reentry.asp** to locate a Reentry Specialist.

Transition from Military to VA
VA has personnel stationed at major military hospitals to help seriously injured Servicemembers returning from Operations Enduring Freedom, Iraqi Freedom, and New Dawn (OEF/OIF/OND) as they transition from military to civilian life. OEF/OIF/OND Servicemembers who have questions about VA benefits or need assistance in filing a VA claim or accessing services can contact the nearest VA office or call 1-800-827-1000.

Transition Assistance Program
This consists of comprehensive workshops at military installations designed to assist Servicemembers as they transition from military to civilian life. The program includes job search, employment and training information, as well as VA benefits information for Servicemembers who are within 18 months of separation or retirement. VA

Benefit Briefings are comprised of two briefings focusing on education, benefits, and VA health care and disability compensation. Servicemembers can sign up for one-on-one appointments with a VA representative. Interested Servicemembers should contact their local TAP Manager to sign up for this program.

VOW to Hire Heroes Act
Improving the Transition Assistance Program (TAP): The **VOW to Hire Heroes Act of 2011** ("the Act") made TAP, including attendance at VA Benefit Briefings, mandatory for most Servicemembers transitioning to civilian status, upgraded career counseling options, and tailored TAP for the 21st Century job market.

Facilitating Seamless Transition
The Act allows Servicemembers to begin the federal employment process prior to separation or retirement from military service. This allows a truly seamless transition from the military to jobs at VA, Department of Homeland Security, and the many other federal agencies seeking to hire Veterans.

Expanding Education and Training
The Act provides nearly 100,000 unemployed Veterans of past eras and wars with up to one year of assistance (equal to the full-time payment rate under the Montgomery GI Bill-Active Duty program) to qualify for jobs in high-demand sectors. It also provides disabled Veterans up to one year of additional Vocational Rehabilitation and Employment benefits.

Translating Military Skills and Training
The Act requires the Department of Labor take a hard look at **military skills and training equivalencies** that are transferrable to the civilian sector, and make it easier to obtain licenses and certifications.

Veterans Tax Credits
The Act provides tax credits for hiring Veterans and disabled Veterans who are out of work

The inTransition
Servicemembers and Veterans may receive assistance from the inTransition Program when they are receiving mental health treatment and are making transitions from military service, location or a health care system. This program provides access to transitional support,

motivation, and healthy lifestyle assistance and advice from qualified coaches through the toll-free telephone number 1-800-424-7877. For more information about the inTransition Program, please log onto **www.health.mil/inTransition**.

Federal Recovery Coordination Program
The Federal Recovery Coordination Program (FRCP), a joint program of DoD and VA, helps coordinate and access federal, state and local programs, benefits and services for seriously wounded, ill, and injured Servicemembers, and their families through recovery, rehabilitation, and reintegration into the community.

Military Services Provide Pre-Separation Counseling
Servicemembers may receive pre-separation counseling 24 months prior to retirement or 12 months prior to separation from active duty. These sessions present information on education, training, employment assistance, National Guard and Reserve programs, medical benefits, and financial assistance.

Verification of Military Experience and Training (VMET)
The VMET Document, DD Form 2586, helps Servicemembers verify previous experience and training to potential employers, negotiate credits at schools, and obtain certificates or licenses. VMET documents are available only through each military branch's support office and are intended for Servicemembers who have at least six months of active service. Servicemembers should obtain VMET documents from their Transition Support Office within 12 months of separation or 24 months of retirement.

Transition Bulletin Board
To find business opportunities, a calendar of transition seminars, job fairs, information on Veterans associations, transition services, training and education opportunities, as well as other announcements visit **www.turbotap.org**.

DoD Transportal
To find locations and phone numbers of all Transition Assistance Offices as well as mini-courses on conducting successful job-search campaigns, writing resumes, using the internet to find a job, and links to job search and recruiting Websites, visit the DoD Transportal at **www.Veteranprograms.com/index.html**.

Veterans' Workforce Investment Program
Recently separated Veterans and those with service-connected disabilities, significant barriers to employment, or who served on active duty during a period in which a campaign or expedition badge was authorized, can contact the nearest state employment office for employment help through the Veterans Workforce Investment Program. The program may be conducted through state or local public agencies, community organizations or private, nonprofit organizations.

State Employment Services
Veterans can find employment information, education and training opportunities, job counseling, job search workshops, and resume preparation assistance at state Workforce Career or One-Stop Centers. These offices also have specialists to help disabled Veterans find employment.

Unemployment Compensation
Veterans who do not begin civilian employment immediately after leaving military service may receive weekly unemployment compensation for a limited time. The amount and duration of payments are determined by individual states. Apply by contacting the nearest state employment office listed in the local telephone directory.

Veterans Preference for Federal Jobs
Since the time of the Civil War, Veterans of the U.S. armed forces have been given some degree of preference in appointments to federal jobs. Veterans' preference in its present form comes from the Veterans' Preference Act of 1944, as amended, and now codified in Title 5, United States Code (U.S.C.). By law, Veterans who are disabled or who served on active duty in the U.S. armed forces during certain specified time periods or in military campaigns are entitled to preference over others when hiring from competitive lists of eligible candidates, and also in retention during a reduction in force (RIF).

To receive preference, a Veteran must have been discharged or released from active duty in the U.S. armed forces under honorable conditions (honorable or general discharge). Preference is also provided for certain widows and widowers of deceased Veterans who died in service, spouses of service-connected disabled Veterans, and mothers of Veterans who died under honorable conditions on active duty or have permanent and total service-connected disabilities. For more information, visit **www.usajobs.gov** or **www.fedshirevets.**

gov.

Veterans' Recruitment Appointment
Allows federal agencies to appoint eligible Veterans to jobs without competition. These appointments can be converted to career or career-conditional positions after two years of satisfactory work. Veterans should apply directly to the agency where they wish to work. For information,www.fedshirevets.gov/.

Small Businesses
VA's Center for Veterans Enterprise helps Veterans interested in forming or expanding small businesses, and helps VA contracting offices identify Veteran-owned small businesses. For information, write the U.S. Department of Veterans Affairs (OOVE), 810 Vermont Avenue, N.W., Washington, DC 20420-0001, call toll-free 1-866-584-2344, or visit **www.vetbiz.gov**. Like other federal agencies, VA is required to place a portion of its contracts and purchases with small and disadvantaged businesses. VA has a special office to help small and disadvantaged businesses get information on VA acquisition opportunities. For information, write the U.S. Department of Veterans Affairs (OOSB), 810 Vermont Avenue, N.W., Washington, DC 20420-0001, call toll-free 1-800-949-8387, or visit **www.va.gov/osdbu/**.

Dependents & Survivors Health Care

Civilian Health and Medical Program of the Department of Veterans Affairs (CHAMPVA). Under CHAMPVA, certain dependents and survivors can receive reimbursement for most medical expenses – inpatient, outpatient, mental health, prescription medication, skilled nursing care and durable medical equipment.

Eligibility: To be eligible for CHAMPVA, an individual cannot be eligible for TRICARE (the medical program for civilian dependents provided by DoD) and must be one of the following:
1. The spouse or child of a Veteran whom VA has rated permanently and totally disabled due to a service-connected disability.
2. The surviving spouse or child of a Veteran who died from a VA-rated service-connected disability, or who, at the time of death, was rated permanently and totally disabled.
3. The surviving spouse or child of a Veteran who died on active

duty service and in the line of duty, not due to misconduct. However, in most of these cases, these family members are eligible for TRICARE, not CHAMPVA.

A surviving spouse under age 55 who remarries loses CHAMPVA eligibility at midnight of the date on remarriage. He/she may re-establish eligibility if the remarriage ends by death, divorce or annulment effective the first day of the month following the termination of the remarriage or December 1, 1999, whichever is later. A surviving spouse who remarries after age 55 does not lose eligibility upon remarriage.

For those who have Medicare entitlement or other health insurance, CHAMPVA is a secondary payer. Beneficiaries with Medicare must be enrolled in Parts A&B to maintain CHAMPVA eligibility. For additional information, contact the Chief Business Office Purchased Care at the VA Health Administration Center, CHAMPVA, P.O. Box 469028, Denver, CO 80246, call 1-800-733-8387 or visit www.va.gov/hac/forbeneficiaries/champva/champva.asp.

Dependents/Survivors and the Health Care Law
The Affordable Care Act, also known as the health care law, was created to expand access to affordable health care coverage to all Americans, lower costs, and improve quality and care coordination. Under the health care law, people will:
• have health coverage that meets a minimum standard (called "minimum essential coverage") by January 1, 2014;
• qualify for an exemption; or
• pay a fee when filing their taxes if they have affordable options but remain uninsured.

Key Information for Family Members about the Health Care Law
• VA wants all Veterans and their families to receive health care that improves their health and well-being.
• Family members are a key part of Veterans' good health and support network.
• Dependents/survivors enrolled in the Civilian Health and Medical Program of the Department of Veterans Affairs (CHAMPVA) or the Spina Bifida Health Care Program meet the requirement to have health care coverage under the health care law and do not need to take any additional steps. The law does not change CHAMPVA or Spina Bifida benefits, access or costs.

Veterans' family members who do not have coverage that meets the health care law's standard should consider their options through the Health Insurance Marketplace, which is a new way to shop for and purchase private health insurance. For more information about the Health Insurance Marketplace, visit **www.healthcare.gov** or call 1-800-318-2596. For additional information about the VA and the health care law, visit **www.va.gov/aca** or call 1-877-222-VETS (8387).

Dependents & Survivors Benefits

Death Gratuity Payment
Military services provide payment, called a death gratuity, in the amount of $100,000 to the next of kin of Servicemembers who die while on active duty (including those who die within 120 days of separation) as a result of service-connected injury or illness.

If there is no surviving spouse or child, then parents or siblings designated as next of kin by the Servicemember may be provided the payment. The payment is made by the last military command of the deceased. If the beneficiary is not paid automatically, application may be made to the military service concerned.

Dependency and Indemnity Compensation
Eligibility: For a survivor to be eligible for **Dependency and Indemnity Compensation** (DIC), one of the following must have directly caused or contributed to the Veteran's death:
1. A disease or injury incurred or aggravated in the line of duty while on active duty or active duty for training.
2. An injury, heart attack, cardiac arrest, or stroke incurred or aggravated in the line of duty while on inactive duty for training.
3. A service-connected disability or a condition directly related to a service-connected disability.

DIC also may be paid to certain survivors of Veterans who were totally disabled from service-connected conditions at the time of death, even though their service-connected disabilities did not cause their deaths. The survivor qualifies if the Veteran was:
1. Continuously rated totally disabled for a period of 10 years immediately preceding death; or

2. Continuously rated totally disabled from the date of military discharge and for at least 5 years immediately preceding death; or
3. A former POW who was continuously rated totally disabled for a period of at least on a year immediately preceding death.

Payments will be offset by any amount received from judicial proceedings brought on by the Veteran's death. When the surviving spouse is eligible for payments under the military's Survivor Benefit Plan (SBP), only the amount of SBP greater than DIC is payable. If DIC is greater than SBP, only DIC is payable. The Veteran's discharge must have been under conditions other than dishonorable.

Payments for Deaths After Jan. 1, 1993: Surviving spouses of Veterans who died on or after Jan. 1, 1993, receive a basic rate, plus additional payments for dependent children, for the aid and attendance of another person if they are patients in a nursing home or require the regular assistance of another person, or if they are permanently housebound.

Special Allowances
Add $261.87 if the Veteran was totally disabled eight continuous years prior to death. Add $266 if there are dependent children under age 18 for the initial two years of entitlement for DIC awards commencing on or after Jan. 1, 2005.

Parents' DIC: VA provides an income-based monthly benefit to the surviving parent(s) of a Servicemember or Veteran whose death was service-related. When countable income exceeds the limit set by law, no benefits are payable. The spouse's income must also be included if living with a spouse.

Restored Entitlement Program for Survivors: Survivors of Veterans who died of service-connected causes incurred or aggravated prior to Aug. 13, 1981, may be eligible for a special benefit payable in addition to any other benefits to which the family may be entitled. The amount of the benefit is based on information provided by the Social Security Administration.

Survivors Pension
VA provides pension benefits to qualifying surviving spouses and unmarried dependent children of deceased Veterans with wartime

service.

Eligibility
To be eligible, spouses must not have remarried (with an exception that remarriage of surviving spouse terminated prior to Nov. 1, 1990), and children must be under age 18, or under age 23 if attending a VA-approved school, or have become permanently incapable of self-support because of disability before age 18. Surviving spouses and children must have qualifying income.

Payment: Survivors pension provides a monthly payment to bring an eligible person's income to a level established by law. The payment is reduced by the annual income from other sources such as Social Security. The payment may be increased if the recipient has unre-imbursed medical expenses that can be deducted from countable income.

Aid and Attendance and Housebound Benefits
Surviving spouses who are eligible for VA survivors pension are eligible for a higher maximum pension rate if they qualify for aid and attendance or housebound benefits. An eligible individual may qualify if he or she requires the regular aid of another person in order to perform personal functions required for everyday living, or is bedridden, a patient in a nursing home due to mental or physical incapacity, blind, or permanently and substantially confined to his/her immediate premises because of a disability.

To apply for aid and attendance or housebound benefits, write to a **VA regional office**. Please include copies of any evidence, preferably a report from an attending physician or a nursing home, validating the need for aid and attendance or housebound type care. The report should contain sufficient detail to determine whether there is disease or injury producing physical or mental impairment, loss of coordination, or conditions affecting the ability to dress and undress, to feed oneself, to attend to sanitary needs, and to keep oneself ordinarily clean and presentable. In addition, it is necessary to determine whether the claimant is confined to the home or immediate premises.

Survivors' & Dependents' Educational Assistance
Eligibility: VA provides educational assistance to qualifying dependents as follows:
    1. The spouse or child of a Servicemember or Veteran who

either died of a service-connected disability, or who has permanent and total service-connected disability, or who died while such a disability existed.

2. The spouse or child of a Servicemember listed for more than 90 days as currently Missing in Action (MIA), captured in the line of duty by a hostile force, or detained or interned by a foreign government or power.

3. The spouse or child of a Servicemember who is hospitalized or receives outpatient care or treatment for a disability that is determined to be totally and permanently disabling, incurred or aggravated due to active duty, and for which the service member is likely to be discharged from military service.

Surviving spouses lose eligibility if they remarry before age 57 or are living with another person who has been recognized publicly as their spouse. They can regain eligibility if their remarriage ends by death or divorce or if they cease living with the person. Dependent children do not lose eligibility if the surviving spouse remarries. Visit **www. benefits.va.gov/gibill** for more information.

Period of Eligibility: The period of eligibility for Veterans' spouses expires 10 years from either the date they become eligible or the date of the Veteran's death. Children generally must be between the ages of 18 and 26 to receive educational benefits. VA may grant extensions to both spouses and children.

The period of eligibility for spouses of Servicemembers who died on active duty expires 20 years from the date of death. This is a change in law that became effective Dec. 10, 2004. Spouses of Servicemembers who died on active duty whose 10-year eligibility period expired before Dec. 10, 2004, now have 20 years from the date of death to use educational benefits.

Training Available: Benefits may be awarded for pursuit of associate, bachelor, or graduate degrees at colleges and universities; independent study; cooperative training; study abroad; certificate or diploma from business, technical, or vocational schools; apprenticeships; on-the-job training programs; farm cooperative courses; and preparatory courses for tests required or used for admission to an institution of higher learning or graduate school.

Benefits for correspondence courses under certain conditions are available to spouses only. Beneficiaries without high-school degrees can pursue secondary schooling, and those with a deficiency in a subject may receive tutorial assistance if enrolled half-time or more.

Special Benefits: Dependents over age 14 with physical or mental disabilities that impair their ability to pursue an education may receive specialized vocational or restorative training, including speech and voice correction, language retraining, lip reading, auditory training, Braille reading and writing, and similar programs. Certain disabled or surviving spouses are also eligible.

Marine Gunnery Sergeant John David Fry Scholarship
Children of those who died in the line of duty on or after Sept. 11, 2001, are potentially eligible to use Post-9/11 GI Bill benefits.

Children of Women Vietnam Veterans Born with Certain Birth Defects: Biological children of women Veterans who served in Vietnam at any time during the period beginning on Feb. 28, 1961, and ending on May 7, 1975, may be eligible for certain benefits because of birth defects associated with the mother's service in Vietnam that resulted in a permanent physical or mental disability.

The covered birth defects do not include conditions due to family disorders, birth-related injuries, or fetal or neonatal infirmities with well-established causes. A monetary allowance is paid at one of four disability levels based on the child's degree of permanent disability.

Appeals of VA Claims Decisions

Veterans and other claimants for VA benefits have the right to appeal decisions made by a VA regional office, medical center or National Cemetery Administration (NCA) office. Typical issues appealed are disability compensation, pension, education benefits, recovery of overpayments, reimbursement for unauthorized medical services, and denial of burial and memorial benefits.

A claimant has one year from the date of the notification of a VA decision to file an appeal. The first step in the appeal process is for a claimant to file a written notice of disagreement with VA regional office, medical center or national cemetery office that made the decision. Following receipt of the written notice, VA will furnish the claimant a "Statement of the Case" describing what facts, laws, and regulations were used in deciding the case.

To complete the request for appeal, the claimant must file a "Substantive Appeal" within 60 days of the mailing of the Statement of the Case, or within one year from the date VA mailed its decision, whichever period ends later.

Board of Veterans' Appeals
The **Board of Veterans' Appeals** ("the Board") makes decisions on appeals on behalf of the Secretary of Veterans Affairs. Although it is not required, a veterans service organization, an agent, or an attorney may represent a claimant. Appellants may present their cases in person to a member of the Board at a hearing in Washington, D.C., at a VA regional office or by videoconference.

Decisions made by the Board can be found at **www.index.va.gov/search/va/bva.html**. The pamphlet, "Understanding the Appeal Process," is available on the website or may be requested by writing: Mail Process Section (014), Board of Veterans' Appeals, 810 Vermont Avenue, NW, Washington, DC 20420.

U.S. Court of Appeals for Veterans Claims
A final Board of Veterans' Appeals decision that does not grant a claimant the benefits desired may be appealed to the **U.S. Court of Appeals for Veterans Claims**. The court is an independent body, not part of the Department of Veterans Affairs.

Notice of an appeal must be received by the court with a postmark that is within 120 days after the Board of Veterans' Appeals mailed its decision. The court reviews the record considered by the Board of Veterans' Appeals. It does not hold trials or receive new evidence. Appellants may represent themselves before the court or have lawyers or approved agents as representatives. Oral argument is held only at the direction of the court. Either party may appeal a decision of the court to the U.S. Court of Appeals for the Federal Circuit and may seek review in the Supreme Court of the United States.

Published decisions, case status information, rules and procedures, and other special announcements can be found at http://www.us-courts.cavc.gov/. The court's decisions can also be found in West's Veterans Appeals Reporter, and on the Westlaw and LEXIS online services. For questions, write the Clerk of the Court, 625 Indiana Ave. NW, Suite 900, Washington, DC 20004, or call (202) 501-5970

Military Medals and Records

Replacing Military Medals
Medals awarded while in active service are issued by the individual military services if requested by Veterans or their next of kin. Requests for replacement medals, decorations, and awards should be directed to the branch of the military in which the Veteran served. However, for Air Force (including Army Air Corps) and Army Veterans, the National Personnel Records Center (NPRC) verifies awards and forwards requests and verification to appropriate services.

Requests for replacement medals should be submitted on Standard Form 180, "Request Pertaining to Military Records," which may be obtained at VA offices or the Internet at www.va.gov/vaforms/. Forms, addresses, and other information on requesting medals can be found on the Military Personnel Records section of NPRC's Website at **www.archives.gov/st-louis/military-personnel/index.html**. For questions, call Military Personnel Records at (314) 801-0800, or e-mail questions to: MPR.center@nara.gov.

When requesting medals, type or clearly print the Veteran's full name, include the Veteran's branch of service, service number or Social Security number, and provide the Veteran's exact or approximate dates of military service. The request must contain the signature of the Veteran or next of kin if the Veteran is deceased. If available, include a copy of the discharge or separation document, WDAGO Form 53-55 or DD Form 214. If discharge or separation documents are lost, Veterans or the next of kin of deceased Veterans may obtain duplicate copies through the eBenefits portal (**www. ebenefits.va.gov**) or by completing forms found on the Internet at **www.archives.gov/research/index.html** and mailing or faxing them to the NPRC.

Alternatively, write the National Personnel Records Center, Military Personnel Records, One Archives Drive, St. Louis, MO 63138-1002. Specify that a duplicate separation document is needed. The Veteran's full name should be printed or typed so that it can be read clearly, but the request must also contain the signature of the Veteran or the signature of the next of kin, if the Veteran is deceased. Include the Veteran's branch of service, service number or Social Security number, and exact or approximate dates and years of service. Use Standard Form 180, "Request Pertaining To Military Records."

It is not necessary to request a duplicate copy of a Veteran's discharge or separation papers solely for the purpose of filing a claim for VA benefits. If complete information about the Veteran's service is furnished on the application, VA will obtain verification of service.

Correcting Military Records
The Secretary of a military department, acting through a **Board for Correction of Military Records**, has authority to change any military record when necessary to correct an error or remove an injustice. A correction board may consider applications for correction of a military record, including a review of a discharge issued by court-martial. Application is made with DD Form 149, available at VA offices, Veterans organizations or visit **www.dtic.mil/whs/directives/infomgt/ forms/formsprogram.htm.**

Review of Discharge from Military Service
Each of the military services maintains a **discharge review board** with authority to change, correct or modify discharges or dismissals not issued by a sentence of a general court-martial. The board has no authority to address medical discharges. If the Veteran is deceased or incompetent, the surviving spouse, next of kin or legal representative, may apply for a review of discharge by writing to the military department concerned, using DD Form 293, "Application for the Review of Discharge from the Armed Forces of the United States." This form may be obtained at a VA regional office, from Veterans organizations or online at **www.dtic.mil/whs/directives/ infomgt/forms/formsprogram.htm.**

However, if the discharge was more than 15 years ago, a Veteran must petition the appropriate Service's Board for Correction of Military Records using DD Form 149, "Application for Correction of Military Records Under the Provisions of Title 10, U.S. Code, Section 1552." A discharge review is conducted by a review of an applicant's record and, if requested, by a hearing before the board.

Discharges awarded as a result of a continuous period of unauthorized absence in excess of 180 days make persons ineligible for

VA benefits regardless of action taken by discharge review boards, unless VA determines there were compelling circumstances for the absence. Boards for the Correction of Military Records also may consider such cases.

Veterans with disabilities incurred or aggravated during active duty may qualify for medical or related benefits regardless of separation and characterization of service. Veterans separated administratively under other than honorable conditions may request that their discharge be reviewed for possible re-characterization, provided they file their appeal within 15 years of the date of separation. Questions regarding the review of a discharge should be addressed to the appropriate discharge review board at the address listed on DD Form 293.

Physical Disability Board of Review
Veterans separated due to disability from Sept. 11, 2001, through Dec. 31, 2009, with a combined rating of 20 percent or less, as determined by the respective branch of service **Physical Evaluation Board** (PEB), and not found eligible for retirement, may be eligible for a review by the Physical Disability Board of Review (PDBR).

The PDBR was established to reassess the accuracy and fairness of certain PEB decisions, and where appropriate, recommend the correction of discrepancies and errors. A PDBR review will not lower the disability rating previously assigned by the PEB, and any correction may be made retroactively to the day of the original disability separation. As a result of the request for review by the PDBR, no further relief from the Board of Corrections of Military Records may be sought, and the recommendation by the PDBR, once accepted by the respective branch of service, is final. A comparison of these two boards, along with other PDBR information, can be viewed at **www.health.mil/pdbr.**

U.S. Department of Health and Human Services
The U.S. Department of Health and Human Services provides funding to states to help low-income households with their heating and home energy costs under the Low Income Home Energy Assistance Program (LIHEAP). LIHEAP can also assist with insulating homes to make them more energy efficient and reduce energy costs. The LIHEAP program in your community determines if your household's income qualifies for the program. To find out where to apply call

1-866-674-6327 or e-mail energy@ncat.org 7 a.m.- 5 p.m. (Mountain Time). More information can be found at **www.acf.hhs.gov/programs/ocs/liheap/#index.html**.

Burial and Memorial Benefits

Veterans discharged from active duty under conditions other than dishonorable; Service members who die while on active duty, active duty for training, or inactive duty training; and spouses and depen dent children of Veterans and active duty service members, may be eligible for VA burial and memorial benefits. (For the purposes of this section, the term "Veteran" includes eligible persons who die during active duty service.) The Veteran does not have to die before a spouse or dependent child can be eligible for burial or memorial benefits. National Guard and reservists who serve the full period for which they are called to active duty, their spouses and dependent children may also be eligible.

Burial in VA National Cemeteries
Burial in a VA national cemetery is available for eligible Veterans, spouses and dependents at no cost and includes the gravesite, grave-liner, opening and closing of the grave, a headstone or marker, and perpetual care as part of a national shrine. For Veterans, ben efits may also include a burial flag, Presidential Memorial Certificate and military funeral honors provided by the Department of Defense.

With certain exceptions, active duty service beginning after Sept 7, 1980, as an enlisted person, and after Oct 16, 1981, as an officer, must be for a minimum of 24 consecutive months or the full period of active duty (as in the case of reservists or National Guard members called to active duty for a limited duration). Active duty for training, by itself, while serving in the reserves or National Guard, is not suf- ficient to confer eligibility. Reservists and National Guard members, as well as their spouses and dependent children, are eligible if they were entitled to retired pay at the time of death, or would have been upon reaching requisite age.

Surviving spouses of Veterans who died on or after Jan. 1, 2000, do not lose eligibility for burial in a national cemetery if they remarry. Unmarried dependent children of Veterans who are under 21 years of age, or under 23 years of age if a full-time student at an approved educational institution, are eligible for burial. Unmarried adult children who become physically or mentally disabled and incapable of self-support before age 21, or age 23 if a full-time student may also be eligible.

Certain parents of Servicemembers who die as a result of hostile activity or from combat training-related injuries may be eligible for burial in a national cemetery with their child. The biological or adopt ed parents of a servicemember who died in combat or while perform ing training in preparation for a combat mission, who leaves no sur viving spouse or dependent child, may be buried with the deceased servicemember if there is available space. Eligibility is limited to servicemembers who died on or after Oct. 7, 2001, and biological or adoptive parents who died on or after Oct. 13, 2010.

The next of kin or authorized representative (e.g., funeral direc-tor) makes interment arrangements at time of need by contacting the National Cemetery Scheduling Office (see **http://www.cem.va.gov/bbene/need.asp**) or, in some cases, the national cemetery in which burial is desired. VA normally does not con duct burials on weekends. Gravesites cannot be reserved; however, VA will honor reservations made before 1973 by the Department of the Army.

VA operates 132 national cemeteries, of which 73 are currently open for both new casket and cremation interments and 18 may accept new interment of cremated remains only. Burial options are limited to those available at a specific cemetery and may include in ground casket, or interment of cremated remains in a columbarium, in-ground, or in a scattering area. Contact the national cemetery directly, or visit our website at **http://www.cem.va.gov.**

Headstones, Markers and Medallions Veterans, active duty ser-vice members, retired Reservists and National Guard service mem-bers, and Reservists and National Guardsmen service members with creditable active duty service, are eligible for an inscribed headstone or marker for their unmarked grave at any cemetery- national, state veterans, tribal, or private. VA will deliver a headstone or marker at no cost, anywhere in the world. For eligible Veterans or service mem-bers buried in a private cemetery whose deaths occurred on or after Nov. 1, 1990, VA may furnish a government headstone or marker (even if the grave is already marked with a private one); or VA may furnish a medallion to affix to an already existing privately-purchased headstone or marker. Spouses and dependent children are eligible for a government head stone or marker only if they are buried in a national or State Veterans cemetery.

Headstones or Markers for private cemeteries: Before ordering, the next of kin or authorized representative should check with the cemetery to ensure that the Government-furnished headstone or marker will be accepted. All installation fees at private cemeteries are the responsibility of the applicant. To submit a claim for a head stone or marker for a gravesite in a private cemetery, use VA Form 40-1330, Application for Standard Government Headstone or Marker (available at http://www.va.gov/vaforms/. A copy of the Veteran's military discharge document is required. Mail forms to Memorial Pro grams Service, Department of Veterans Affairs, 5109 Russell Road, Quantico, VA 22134-3903. The form and supporting documents may also be faxed toll free to 1-800-455-7143.

To submit a claim for a head stone or marker for a gravesite in a private cemetery, use VA Form 40-1330, Application for Standard Government Headstone or Marker (available at **http://www.va.gov/ vaforms/**. A copy of the Veteran's military discharge document is required. Mail forms to Memorial Pro grams Service, Department of Veterans Affairs, 5109 Russell Road, Quantico, VA 22134-3903. The form and supporting documents may also be faxed toll free to 1-800-455-7143.

"In Memory Of" Markers: VA provides memorial headstones and markers with "In Memory Of" as the first line of inscription for those whose remains have not been recovered or identified, were buried at sea, donated to science or cremated and scattered. Eligibility is the same as for regular headstones and markers.

Inscriptions: Headstones and markers must be inscribed with the name of the deceased, branch of service, and year of birth and death. They also may be inscribed with other optional information, including an emblem of belief and, space permitting, additional text including military rank; war service such as "World War II;" complete dates of birth and death; military awards; military organizations; civilian or Veteran affiliations; and personalized words of endearment.

Medallion in lieu of government headstone or marker for private cemeteries: For Veterans or service members whose death occurred on or after Nov. 1, 1990, VA is authorized to provide a me dallion instead of a headstone or marker if the grave is in a private cemetery and already marked with a privately-purchased headstone or marker.

To submit a claim for a medallion to be affixed to a private head-stone/marker in a private cemetery, use VA Form 40-1330M, Claim for Government Medallion (available at **http://www.va.gov/vaforms**). A copy of the Veteran's military discharge document is required. Mail forms to Memorial Programs Service, Department of Veterans Affairs, 5109 Russell Road, Quantico, VA 22134-3903. The form and supporting documents may also be faxed toll free to 1-800-455-7143.

To check the status of a claim for a headstone or marker for place ment in a national, state, or tribal Veterans cemetery, please call the cemetery. To check the status of one being placed in a private cemetery, please contact the Applicant Assistance Unit at 1-800-697-6947 or via email at mps.headstones@va.gov.

Other Memorialization
Presidential Memorial Certificates are issued to recognize the miltary service of honorably discharged deceased Veterans and per sons who died in the active military, naval, or air service. Next of kin, relatives and other loved ones may apply for a certificate by mailing, or faxing a completed and signed VA Form 40-0247, Presidential Memorial Certificate Request Form (available at http://www.va.gov/vaforms), along with a copy of the Veteran's military discharge documents or proof of honorable military service. The processing of requests sent without supporting documents will be delayed until eligibility can determined. Eligibility requirements can be found at **http://www.cem.va.gov**.

Burial Flags: Generally, VA will furnish a U.S. burial flag to memori alize Veterans who received other than dishonorable discharge. This includes certain persons who served in the organized military forces of the Commonwealth of the Philippines while in service of the U.S armed forces and who died on or after April 25, 1951. Also eligible for a burial flag are Veterans who were entitled to retired pay for ser-vice in the Reserve or National Guard, or would have been entitled if over age 60; and members or former members of the Selected Reserve who served their initial obligation, or were discharged for a disability incurred or aggravated in the line of duty, or died while a

58

member of the Selected Reserve. The next of kin may apply for the flag at any VA Regional Office or U.S. Post Office by completing VA Form 21-2008, Application for United States Flag for Burial Purposes (available at **http://www.va.gov/vaforms/**). In most cases, a funeral director will help the family obtain the flag.

Reimbursement of Burial Expenses: VA will pay a burial allowance up to $2,000 if the Veteran's death is service-connected. In such cases, the person who bore the Veteran's burial expenses may claim reimbursement from VA. In some cases, VA will pay the cost of transporting the remains of a Veteran whose death was service-connected to the nearest national cemetery with available gravesites. There is no time limit for filing reimbursement claims in service-connected death cases.

Burial Allowance: VA will pay a burial and funeral allowance of up to $2,000 for Veterans who die from service-connected injuries. VA will pay a burial and funeral allowance of up to $300 for Veterans who, at the time of death from nonservice-connected injuries were entitled to receive pension or compensation or would have been entitled if they were not receiving military retirement pay. VA will pay a burial and funeral allowance of up to $734 when the Veteran's death occurs in a VA facility, a VA-contracted nursing home or a state Veterans nursing home. In cases in which the Veteran's death was not service con nected, claims must be filed within two years after burial or crema tion.

Plot Allowance: VA will pay a plot allowance of up to $734 when a Veteran is buried in a cemetery not under U.S. government jurisdiction if: the Veteran was discharged from active duty because of disability incurred or aggravated in the line of duty; the Veteran was receiving compensation or pension or would have been if the Veteran was not receiving military retired pay; or the Veteran died in a VA facility. The plot allowance may be paid to the state for the cost of a plot or interment in a state-owned cemetery reserved solely for Veteran burials if the Veteran is buried without charge. Burial expenses paid by the deceased's employer or a state agency will not be reimbursed.

For more information about burial and memorial benefits contact the nearest national cemetery (http://www.va.gov/directory/guide/division.asp?dnum=4&isFlash=0), call1-202-632-8035, or visit website at www.cem.va.gov/.

Veterans Cemeteries Administered by Other Agencies Department of the Army: Administers Arlington National Cemetery and other Army installation cemeteries. Eligibility is generally more restrictive than at VA national cemeteries. For information, call (703) 607-8000, write Superintendent, Arlington National Cemetery, Arlington, VA 22211, or visit **www.arlingtoncemetery.mil/**.

State and Tribal Veterans Cemeteries: There are currently 95 VA grant-funded Veterans cemeteries operating in 45 states and U.S. Territories that offer burial options for Veterans and their families. VA grant-funded cemeteries have similar eligibility requirements and certain states/tribal organizations may require state or tribal residency/membership. Some services, particularly for family members, may require a fee. Contact the state or tribal Veterans cemetery or the state Veterans Affairs office for information. To locate a state or tribal Veterans cemetery, visit www.cem.va.gov/grants/veterans_cemeteries.asp

Unclaimed Veterans Remains: "Unclaimed Veterans" are a defined as those who die with no next of kin to claim their remains and insufficient funds to cover burial expenses. A VA pension or other compensation is no longer a pre-requisite for these "Unclaimed Veterans" to receive monetary burial benefits. In addition to burial in a VA national, state or tribal Veterans cemetery and a government headstone or marker, there are monetary benefits associated with burial of unclaimed Veterans remains.

These monetary benefits include reimbursement for the cost of the casket or urn used for burial, reimbursement for transportation to a national cemetery, a burial allowance and a plot allowance. More information on memorial and monetary burial benefits for unclaimed Veteran remains can be found at http://www.cem.va.gov/CEM/docs/FactSheets/Unclaimed_remains.pdf. For Veterans who die while at a VA facility under authorized VA admission or at a non-VA facility under authorized VA admission, and are unclaimed, the closest VA healthcare facility is responsible for arranging proper burial for the unclaimed Veteran.